PREFACE

The photographers who can successfully capture and convey the essence of a particular garden can be counted on the fingers of a single hand!

Garden photography is a highly specialized art form, and requires not only an understanding of aesthetics and architectural principles—landscape and otherwise—but also a thorough understanding of what a garden is all about as it rings the season's changes. Above all, it takes consummate patience along with a flexibility that embraces rising with the dawn and foregoing dinner until the sun has set. Not only should the garden element be captured at its apogee, but the light must be just so and the breeze nonexistent. It can take several days before the conditions are just right—more than often, maddeningly, only for the briefest instant.

Ideally, the photograph should convey a sense of place, evoking the feelings one would have walking through the setting, almost to the point of intimating its unreproducible scents and sounds and capturing its numinous quality.

Mick Hales is one of the accomplished handful of garden photographers who succeed in this demanding profession, and, as a consequence, are invited to photograph gardens wherever they may be. In *Gardens Around the World: 365 Days*, we are privileged to accompany Mick as he leads us through more than 150 gardens—from the Alhambra to Zelun, a tiny Sino-Tibetan hamlet beyond the Wolong Valley west of Chengdu. While roughly two-thirds of the gardens are North American, the gardens of the United Kingdom, France, South and Central America, and Asia are represented as well.

Some of these gardens are well known. Others are new to us, but each garden is unique and filled with ideas that we can learn from and adapt to our own surroundings. The ensemble splendidly illustrates the universality of the genre.

John Dixon Hunt has said: "Places tell stories to those who will listen and listeners are helped by the translator." This colorful and moving collection of garden photographs proves the point that not only are the creators of the gardens in question translators but, most important, so are the talented professionals who convey their essence in such accessible form!

Frank Cabot,   November 16, 2003

MICK HALES

GARDENS AROUND THE WORLD: 365 DAYS

TEXT AND PHOTOGRAPHS BY MICK HALES

PREFACE BY FRANK CABOT

HARRY N. ABRAMS, INC., PUBLISHERS

INTRODUCTION

Gardens Around the World: 365 Days is a celebration of gardens each day of the year and one day at a time. It celebrates gardens from the grandest to the most humble. The selection is quite random, in that they were photographed over a period of twenty years for a variety of people and purposes. The images chosen are not necessarily definitive pictures of these gardens, more a taste or a reflection of their full beauty that requires us to go further with our own imaginations. The result, though, is a powerful testament to man's constant interaction with God's creative nature within himself and the plants around him.

People and gardens are always changing, which gives a particular moment in a garden significance. The very transient nature of gardens is both strength and weakness, as it is with all living things—including ourselves. Often, the relationship between gardener and garden is so personal that it cannot be passed on at his or her death, unless someone has been trained who really understands the gardener's vision. But even if the direction is held true, the garden must and will change. To add to the challenge, the gardener is offered an extraordinary variety of plants for his palette of color, form, and hardiness; deciding which plant to use where can be a lifelong endeavor.

What makes people want to garden, as they have done since the beginning of recorded history? Many people must garden to put food on the table—the most basic of our human needs. Some gardens are made solely to provide flowers for arrangements indoors. Some people garden to work through psychological stress or heal emotional wounds. Monks, nuns, and laypeople have used gardens for prayer and meditation for centuries. Some gardens are used as status symbols of the owners' wealth and significance, with the actual work done by hired help. Herbal or physic gardens were the health systems for communities up to quite recently. For some, the garden is purely an extension of the house, with an outside grill and piped music as entertainment. For many, it is a canvas for a living art form with lines, shapes, and colors created by trees, water, and flowers. Botanic gardens are for learning and classification of the flora in our world. Some people garden just because their parents or grandparents did, and it is simply a part of life. There are many reasons to garden, but there is a common experience throughout—the gardener shares in the absolute mystery of creation.

As the gardener's hands dig into the soil and the smell of humus is released, he joins in an experience our ancestors undertook at the beginning of humanity. When bulbs push up their green shoots through snow in the spring and open to brilliantly colored flowers, surely one has to ask, how did this all come about to work so beautifully? When flowers are arranged inside and one can study closely the complexity of their design and the purity of their color, one has to ask again, how did this come about? So it has been for all generations. Through their engagement with the mystery of creation, gardeners experience life more fully. This fundamental interaction is what makes gardens so important throughout the world.

Indeed, gardens have caused people to fight over them, villages have been removed to enhance the view for them, rivers have been diverted, tunnels created, lakes dug. Men have risked their lives collecting plants for them. Gardens can get into one's life with a passion that grows year after year. So it is appropriate that we think about them and record them, for they are, after all, a part of the fabric of our society.

In all art forms, a few works stand out as classics. This is also true of gardens, but unlike a painting or sculpture, a garden is always changing and cannot be traded. It must be experienced as a place unto itself, in a time and season that cannot be held still, with daylight that will not stand still. The garden photographer learns that a particular image may only exist for minutes before it is gone forever, but remembering the feeling one had while being there can last a lifetime. Society has learned, too, that gardens are significant, and that the better ones should be preserved, where possible, for people to experience after their creators have passed on. The National Trust in England and the Garden Conservancy in America, as well as others throughout the world, have taken up this daunting but valuable task.

As our society moves faster and faster, with technological advances each year, it is hard for us to keep our connection to the land. Keeping a garden is one answer to this loss—having one's hands in and smelling the soil. Watching plants grow, flower, and die back reminds us of our own humanity and the lives we have been given.

1

THE ABKHAZI GARDEN

VICTORIA, BRITISH COLUMBIA

The Abkhazi Garden is known for its low, clipped azaleas, curving lawns edged with heather, its mature rhododendrons, and its broom hybrids—all growing out of a love affair that lasted over sixty years. The love affair began in Paris in the 1920s, when Prince Nicholas Abkhazi, a Georgian exile, met Marjorie (Peggy) Pemberton-Carter. Separated by family obligations and World War II, both suffered imprisonment as prisoners of war, Peggy in Shanghai and Nicholas in Germany. After the war they met again in Canada, and married. In 1946, they purchased land in a suburb of Victoria and immediately began to garden while living in a modest garden shed as their house was being built. The garden is now in trust to the Land Conservancy of British Columbia, which, along with friends and neighbors, valiantly raised funds to save it from development. The many different small gardens with their Japanese maples and flowering shrubs, carefully pruned to fold into large granite outcrops, reveal Princess Peggy Abkhakzi's very personal eye.

2

AGECROFT HALL
RICHMOND, VIRGINIA

Agecroft Hall, a Tudor manor house, was moved stone by stone in the 1920s from the Irwell River in Lancashire, England, to the James River in Richmond, Virginia. The landscape architect Charles Gillette created several gardens for it, among them a series of brick-walled terraces descending toward the river. The beds on one terrace hold a collection of plants recorded by John Tradescant the Younger, who, commissioned by King Charles I, visited Virginia on a plant-hunting expedition in the 1630s.

AGECROFT HALL

RICHMOND, VIRGINIA

Every spring, thousands of tulips bloom along with the azaleas that border the pool-centered sunken garden. When the tulips have finished flowering, they will be replaced by summer annuals. Agecroft's commitment to its Tudor origins is also evoked in an Elizabethan knot garden.

4

AIRDRIE FARM
BLUEGRASS REGION, KENTUCKY

Airdrie Farm has an original Jens Jensen (1860–1951) landscape garden commissioned by W.E. Simms. Some might say that it is just trees and not a garden at all, and that would probably have pleased the strong-willed Viking landscape architect. The landscape may seem as if it just happened, but Jensen's combinations of trees and his placement of them to catch the sun's rays for maximum effect is carefully calculated. Here, the dark green of a fir sets off to perfection the golden autumn leaves of a ginkgo. Jensen did not often plant exotic trees like the ginkgo, but he included them in his design if they were already on the site or the owner particularly wanted them.

AIRDRIE FARM

BLUEGRASS REGION, KENTUCKY

Jensen believed in the civilizing power of nature and was an ardent conservationist. He had studied the Midwest landscape carefully, and became its passionate defender and a member of what is called the Prairie School of design. His landscapes always take their inspiration from the vegetation and geology of their local environment. At Airdrie, the broad belts of trees and open lawns are stylized versions of the pre-Columbian native woods and buffalo-mowed grasslands.

6

AIRDRIE FARM
BLUEGRASS REGION, KENTUCKY

In summer, within the tree groves, carpets of *Geranium maculatum* and *Hesperis matronalis* stretch as far as the eye can see. Jensen understood and wherever possible re-created the layering of canopy trees, understory trees, shrubs, and wildflowers typical of woodlands in much of the United States.

THE ALHAMBRA AND GENERALIFE GARDENS

GRANADA, SPAIN

Myth and romance cling to the walls of La Alhambra, "The Red." This complex of palaces and fortifications, gardens and fountains, courtyards and belvederes, which spreads along a cliff overlooking the city of Granada on one side and the Sierra Nevada range on the other, was begun by the founder of the Nasrid sultanate in the thirteenth century. Most of what remains today, like the palace of the Partal, seen here from its gardens, was built by his descendants in the fourteenth century. In 1492, the last Moorish ruler, Boabdil, surrendered to Ferdinand and Isabella, bringing to an end Mohammedan Spain.

THE ALHAMBRA AND GENERALIFE GARDENS

GRANADA, SPAIN

Perched on top of the Cerra del Sol or Hill of the Sun above the Alhambra is the Generalife, the summer palace of the sultans. In both palaces the sight and sound of water is a constant, a heritage of the desert origins of the Moorish people. The famous arching jets of the Patio de la Acequia are in fact a nineteenth-century addition, but the structure of the garden, a long narrow pool flanked by flowerbeds and enclosed on all sides by arcades, is faithful to its origins.

THE ALHAMBRA AND GENERALIFE GARDENS

GRANADA, SPAIN

The walkway vaulted with roses on one of the Generalife's terraces is a twentieth-century creation, but it echoes the arcades, the door and window arches of Moorish architecture, and the love of roses so often expressed in Moorish poetry.

THE ALHAMBRA AND GENERALIFE GARDENS

GRANADA, SPAIN

The central fountain in the Patio de Daraxa, a vestige of the ancient interior garden of the Alhambra, is antique and Islamic, but the hedged parterres and the planting—cypresses, orange trees, and roses—date from its restoration in the 1920s.

11

THE ALHAMBRA AND GENERALIFE GARDENS

GRANADA, SPAIN

Originally, the terraces that step down the hill from the palace of the Generalife were filled with orchards and kitchen gardens to supply the court, and the pools were *acequias*, or irrigation canals. In the mid-twentieth century, the restorers chose to fill the terraces with pleasure gardens.

12

THE ALHAMBRA AND GENERALIFE GARDENS

GRANADA, SPAIN

The pools, basins, and jets on this terrace at the Generalife are clearly inspired by the Patio de la Acequia, but its walls are tall, precisely clipped hedges and arches of cypress with more cypresses, unclipped, as accents.

13

ASTICOU AZALEA GARDEN
NORTHEAST HARBOR, MAINE

A harmonious blend of three kinds of Japanese garden—a raked sand and rock meditation garden; a stroll garden of streams, ponds, and azaleas; and a small moss garden—Asticou was created by Charles Savage in 1956, when his friend the noted garden designer Beatrix Farrand decided to dismantle her own estate. Savage, who owned the Asticou Inn, offered to make a new home for her plants. Selecting an alder swamp close by the inn, he designed the garden, had the ground prepared and the trees and shrubs planted, all within a year. In spite of the normal changes and revisions that a garden undergoes over time, this evocation of Japan by a man who had never been there and took his inspiration from books remains a remarkable achievement and is lovingly maintained by volunteers.

THE BACON GARDEN

MONTECITO, CALIFORNIA

Two white chairs are placed at the focal point of a magical vista framed by dark evergreen trees and pampas grass. Just in front of the chairs is a small reflecting pool at a lower level; then a larger pool on a second terrace; and finally, a large oval reflecting pool with a lawn encircled by large pine trees. The distant mountains, which turn orange with the sunset, complete the vista, and all is reflected back to the focal point and the two white chairs. Russell Page said a garden cannot compete with a landscape; that one must either enclose the garden or lose it. There are places where endorsing the landscape is enough. This is an old name for a property that has now changed hands.

BAGATELLE PARK

Now best known for the rose gardens added to it in 1906, the Bagatelle park in the Bois de Boulogne was originally laid out in 1777 as a romantic landscape garden by the Scots designer Thomas Blaikie. His patron was the Comte d'Artois, brother of Louis XVI, who had boasted to his sister-in-law, Marie Antoinette, that he could build a palace and gardens for her in two months. She bet that it was impossible. The count employed 900 workmen day and night to win the wager.

16

BAGATELLE PARK

PARIS, FRANCE

Not only are the roses of Bagatelle displayed in a variety of imaginative ways—tree roses trained in parasols, roses climbing arches and smothering pillars—but the park is also the home of an annual competition to find the best new garden roses. Almost equally spectacular in its season is the Iris Garden, added by the distinguished garden designer J.-C. N. Forestier, who was instrumental in saving the park in 1905.

17

BAGATELLE PARK

PARIS, FRANCE

Over the centuries, Bagatelle has had many owners and undergone many changes, narrowly escaping destruction several times. Quite remarkably, however, some vestiges of Blaikie's original creation survive—the broad lawns and specimen trees as well as the picturesque rock-work cascade and its pool.

BALLYMALOE HERB GARDEN

KINOITH, IRELAND

In the quiet of the County Cork countryside, Ballymaloe Inn and Cookery School stands out as a beacon of culinary excellence. Myrtle Allen and her daughter Darina champion the virtues of fresh Irish produce brought right from the gardens and fields around them, preparing them with a sophisticated Irish simplicity that draws Frenchmen from Paris. Inspired by the vegetable garden at Vilandry, in France, it contains some seventy different herbs within a boxwood edging.

BALLYMALOE HERB GARDEN

KINOITH, IRELAND

More vertical standing plants like angelica, globe artichokes, lovage, and cardoons are placed in the centers of the beds, and a viewing platform built in one corner allows one to sit and look down over the parterres of herbs. The garden is enclosed by a reinvigorated beech hedge that is part of an older garden laid out circa 1870 with two more enclosed spaces of the same size. The herbs are planted by contrasting colors and include lemon balm, bronze fennel, purple sage, summer savory, lovage, garlic, chives, lemon verbena, and sweet cicely. There are two beds devoted to mints, among them Moroccan, apple, chocolate, ginger, and spearmint.

20

BARNSLEY HOUSE

Barnsley House was built in 1697 of Cotswold stone and is the backdrop for Rosemary Verey's quintessential English garden. Verey came to gardening relatively late in life but more than made up for it, leaving a gardening legacy that continues to influence gardeners on both sides of the Atlantic. For all its originality, the garden reflects Verey's great knowledge of garden history. One example is the yew-lined walk of interplanted Cotswold stone that leads from the house to a view of the surrounding wall.

21

BARNSLEY HOUSE
CIRENCESTER, ENGLAND

Barnsley, with little more than three acres of garden, is enough to lose oneself in. There are the famous Laburnum Walk, underplanted with alliums; the yew-lined path of interplanted Cotswold stone; the knot garden; the pleached tree walk; the deep herbaceous borders; hedges of roses; potted plants around the front door, and, of course, Rosemary Verey's kitchen garden. All have been reinterpreted in gardens from the Cotswolds to Tennessee.

BARNSLEY HOUSE

CIRENCESTER, ENGLAND

The kitchen garden, also called the potager—the French name indicating that it has been laid out to be ornamental as well as productive—sports a metal tunnel wreathed in zucchini and sweet peas, underplanted in summer with sunflowers and rudbeckias. In another area, a small wooden arbor with a white seat faces the center of a circle of lavender, with eight standard white roses anchoring boxwood-edged beds of onions, cabbages, lettuces, artichokes, beets, carrots, red-stemmed chard, brussels sprouts, and herbs. The onion leaves are all laid flat to the ground in the same direction, adding to the formality of the design.

23

THE BENTLEY AND LA ROSA GARDEN

BUCKS COUNTY, PENNSYLVANIA

On a steep hill with a distant view of the Delaware River, the country home of New York architects Ron Bentley and Sal La Rosa has been quietly growing. The desire for the various elements to blend with the land is articulated by the tool shed that sits on the steep driveway with its tall dry-stone wall front topped off with ferns and a roof of verdant sod. The garden and pool are placed some distance from the house, to achieve a southern exposure and good views. Curving stone steps offset the straight lines of the pool and are planted with the grays of sage, *Artemsia* 'Silver Mound,' and *Stachys byzantina,* which complement the color of the pool stone. A large cedar post anchors the pool house roof, which follows the angle of the land behind. Sea foam roses soften the stone retaining wall and are the first flowers to catch the morning light.

THE BIESENKAMP MOSS GARDEN

CHERRY HILL, NEW JERSEY

In Dr. Jack Biesenkamp's garden, a green sheet of moss extends through the whole garden, uninterrupted except by shadows from the tall oak trees. Here and there a river of flat pebbles meanders across the green. This is the garden's strength—the way the shadows move over the smooth surface, how the moss shades to a darker green in the rain, how it feels to walk on it barefoot.

BILTMORE ESTATE

George W. Vanderbilt opened Biltmore for a family Christmas in 1895, and it must have made quite an impression. The house was designed by architect Richard Morris Hunt in the elaborately detailed style of a French chateau. The property covered some 125,000 acres, and the famous landscape architect Fredrick Law Olmsted (1822–1903) was commissioned to design an appropriate approach to the house and grounds around it. Olmsted suggested that Vanderbilt treat much of the land as managed forest, and Gifford Pinchot took on that responsibility. It became the starting point for the U.S. Forest Service. A stand of pampas grass is all that is left in one of the cutting gardens as the winter draws in.

26

BILTMORE ESTATE

ASHEVILLE, NORTH CAROLINA

Olmsted worked on the three-mile approach road to the house with a careful planting of deciduous and pine tree seedlings native to North Carolina. He sculpted the landscapes that were visible from the house, and created a lake at the bottom of the hill behind it. To the right of the house, he laid out an appropriately formal Italianate garden, and in front of the house a long uphill vista. The four-acre walled garden is planted with large blocks of color in front of a conservatory. The gardens—a spring garden and an azalea garden—gradually become more informal as you move away from the house, with a bass pond and woodland and lake walks.

27

A BIRMINGHAM GARDEN

ALABAMA

This garden was designed by Mary Zahl and is several gardens in one. The front of the brick house has boxwood scrolled on both sides of a stone terrace. A wooden canopy covered with climbing roses shades an upper level of the terrace. Gray stone squares are placed to leave a gap in which fine grass grows, creating an accented pattern on the floor. A secluded garden behind the house has an oval perennial border with mellow shades of silver, blue, and pink. Next to this garden is a swimming pool with magnolia and boxwood bones, highlighted with violas and snapdragons. The stones of the pool terrace are also separated with grass between as in the front of the house, and the theme is developed further at the entrance to the pool garden. Instead of grass, *Pratia pedunculata* is here set between the stones, recalling the entry passage. White and yellow violas mixed with ferns finish off the simple color palette. A homogeneous design runs throughout.

28

BLAIRSDEN

NEW JERSEY

Blairsden stands out as an American garden with American plantings in an Italianate form. The house, by the architects Carrère and Hastings, was completed in 1903 for Clinton Ledyard Blair, whose fortune came from banking and railroads. The landscape architect James Greenleaf, also known for his work on the Lincoln Memorial in Washington, laid out the gardens with grand strokes into the hilltop site. From the front of the house, a grand stairway with falling fountains flanked by dogwood trees directs the eye to the Bernardsville Mountains. A boxwood hedge follows the descending stairway and a rill runs down the center, feeding the fountains at each terrace.

29

BLAKE GARDEN

Two sisters working together designed the Blake Garden, which is now a part of the University of California. Anita Day Symmes Blake and Mabel Symmes—one of the first landscape architects to graduate from Berkeley—created an Italianate garden to suit the house designed by Walker Bliss in the 1920s. A long reflecting pool culminates in a double stairway flanked by two juniper trees. Rock outcroppings are dressed with a wide assortment of flowers.

BLAKE GARDEN
KENSINGTON, CALIFORNIA

A cutting garden surrounds a square pool with dahlias, carnations, roses, hollyhocks, larkspurs, and Sweet Williams. Anita Blake was an avid collector of plants, and through seed exchange increased the cultivated plants in the garden to about 2,500. The end result is a scientifically significant garden appropriate for the University of California, with specimens of dawn redwoods from China, Himalayan dogwoods, New Zealand lacebarks, African corn lilies, and Guernsey lilies.

31

BRANDOLINI GARDEN

ITALY

Count Brando Brandolini D'Adda loves open green gardens and was inspired, with the help of Russell Page, to landscape the family gardens at Vistorta. Vistorta is a working farm and vineyard producing an excellent merlot, and the count wanted a garden appropriate to a working estate. Russell Page introduced a series of gravity-fed lakes and arranged trees to direct vistas. Water-loving plants, like iris, are placed on the surrounds of the lake, but only there, so the lush grass lawn remains free of flowerbeds.

1

BRANDOLINI GARDEN
ITALY

Roses are used in all kinds of imaginative ways, and different varieties of the same color are combined to achieve the height and density desired. Here a repeat-blooming white rose is trained against the wall of a farm building. An island on one of the lakes has white roses mounded right to the water so that they reflect in it. Follies made of white stone turrets are surrounded by water and covered with climbing white roses.

2

BRANT GARDEN

CONNECTICUT

The Brant garden bears the stamp of two designers, Russell Page and Deborah Nevins. The forecourt and outlying landscape were designed by Page with pleached trees, gravel, lawn, and yew hedges. A central grass island in the forecourt has a large tulip poplar, which dominates the trees surrounding the house. Deborah Nevins designed an oblong garden enclosed with hedges, which at the far end form a semicircle. On either side of the garden lie deep perennial borders reminiscent of Gertrude Jekyll (1843–1932), with large groupings of perennials in purples, pinks, and whites.

3

BRANT GARDEN
CONNECTICUT

This garden is overlooked by a stone terrace. Lutyens-like circular steps connect the two levels and reflect back to the circular hedge at the end of the garden. The warm colors of the dianthus and tunic flowers join the pinks of the peonies in the border to bring the two levels together.

BRIEF

The landscape gardener, writer, and art collector Bevis Bawa names his house Brief—a clue to his intellect, humor, and the sharpness of his thinking. In the 1950s and 1960s he wrote a gardening column for the *Ceylon Daily News* titled "Briefly by Bevis," with a satirical take on the British presence. The garden at Brief is also full of plays on ideas and visual juxtapositions. By combining classical garden archetypes with tropical plantings, he places this Sri Lankan garden closer to Versailles than to Colombo.

5

IL BROLINO
MONTECITO, CALIFORNIA

The lumber heiress Mary Stewart commissioned Florence Yoch to design her garden in 1922. Yoch and her partner, Lucille Council, together designed some 250 gardens from the 1920s into the 1960s. They received several commissions from women, and a Greek temple garden for Dorothy Arzner became an introduction to the movie business. Many movie landscapes followed, including those for *Gone with the Wind*. The Mary Stewart house is dramatically placed, with the Santa Ynez Mountains to the north and the Pacific Ocean to the south. A formal topiary garden with multiple animal and bird shapes comprises the main garden.

6

IL BROLINO

MONTECITO, CALIFORNIA

Yoch's attention to detail and her ability to combine many experiences at once are evident at Il Brolino. The clipped hedges of the topiary garden and the grass parterres of the nearby wellhead garden contrast with an informal seating area shaded by a magnificent oak tree.

7

IL BROLINO
MONTECITO, CALIFORNIA

A major axis leads up from the house to a fountain inspired by the one at the Villa Medici in Rome and a monumental exedra, which focus the view of the mountains behind. The asymmetrical placement of the tall eucalyptus was a deliberate stroke that animates the design. Il Brolino has the drama of a movie set, even though it was designed before Yoch's movie career began.

8

BURFORD PRIORY
THE COTSWOLDS, ENGLAND

In the heart of the Cotswolds, hidden from the bustle of the town of Burford, sits the Priory. The main house, which dates back to the end of the sixteenth century, has an imposing front but is well screened from the town with perimeter tree plantings. A wall encloses the property two-thirds of the way around, with the River Windrush bordering its remaining flank. The property was taken over for monastic purposes in 1949 by the sisters of the Community of the Salutation of St. Mary and later adopted the Benedictine rule. In 1987, it became a double monastery of monks and nuns.

BURFORD PRIORY

THE COTSWOLDS, ENGLAND

The garden is an English country house garden adapted to monastic needs. Within the monastic enclosure there is a walled formal garden with robust topiaries running parallel to the side of the main house.

BURFORD PRIORY
THE COTSWOLDS, ENGLAND

The sculpted form of an old mulberry tree anchors one corner opposite the Elizabethan Chapel of St. John in the other. Behind the walled garden is the monastery's cemetery, and beyond it a woodland with many options for sylvan walks.

ROBERTO BURLE MARX

RIO DE JANEIRO, BRAZIL

Roberto Burle Marx (1909–1995) always extensively decorated his garden and the various buildings of his estate outside of Rio, *Sitio Santo Antonio da Bica*, for his birthday with sculptures he made out of various plant materials. Widely credited as the creator of the modern garden, he was also a driving force in nature conservation. He was a plant explorer throughout his life, and several species are named after him—behind the house a large, shaded structure housed plants from his many trips to the Amazon forest. He had at least 3,000 works of landscape design to his credit, but his creative energy also came out in painting and music.

12

ROBERTO BURLE MARX

RIO DE JANEIRO, BRAZIL

Whenever he could, Burle Marx rescued granite architectural elements from eighteenth- and early-nineteenth-century buildings that were being demolished in the course of Rio's modernization, and recycled them in his designs. He assembled some of those fragments to create a fountain wall at one end of the garden on the veranda side of his house, a wall that also screens out the driveway.

13

ROBERTO BURLE MARX
RIO DE JANEIRO, BRAZIL

On the other side of the house, rectangular beds mulched with boulders display a collection of vrieseas, velozias, and bromelias. These dramatic tropical plants grow on mountainsides, get most of their nourishment from the rainwater they collect in their leaf rosettes, and demand good drainage.

ROBERTO BURLE MARX

RIO DE JANEIRO, BRAZIL

His 1948 landscape for Odette Monteiro has become an icon of modern landscape architecture. He moved earth to create a lake that reflects the wonderful sugarloaf mountains beyond. Pathways and large drifts of massed tropical foliage pull the eye to the horizon. Characterized by similar flowing forms, his urban work, exemplified by Flamengo Park—which runs along Rio de Janeiro's seafront—and commercial work like the Safra Bank in Saõ Paulo, have influenced landscape design around the world.

CHELSEA PHYSIC GARDEN
LONDON, ENGLAND

The Chelsea Physic Garden is one of the bastions of botanic history and still functions today as an educational institution. It was founded in 1673 as the Apothecaries' Garden, with the function of teaching plant identification. Its location close to the Thames eased the transportation of plant material and provided a warmer microclimate. It has always been involved with seed sharing, and by the 1700s had initiated an international seed exchange system that is still operating. The garden is divided into different areas of interest, with a large portion still involved with pharmaceutical plants; perfumery and aromatherapy; a garden of world medicine; and rare and unusual vegetables. Then there is a historical walk, which has plants associated with many of the prominent figures of the Chelsea Physic's past. There are also beds of plants planted by botanical order. A part of the garden is dedicated to the plants of the Atlantic islands—the list goes on and on. This is a garden for the serious plantsman.

16

CHESTERWOOD

The summer studio of sculptor Daniel Chester French (1850–1931), designed by architect Henry Bacon, sits on 122 acres of the Berkshire Hills. French, who created *The Minute Man* and the *Seated Lincoln* for the Lincoln Memorial in Washington, D.C., was always concerned about the context of his sculpture—what it stood on and what was close by. This is reflected in the garden around his studio, which is a mixture of Italianate and naturalistic elements. An allée of standard hydrangeas draws the eye to the studio doors, where the current piece he was working on could be seen. Behind the hydrangea allée is a dense wood with Doric columns signaling the change from a formal to an informal setting. On the far side of the studio, a grand vista across to the mountains completes the setting.

FEBRUARY

17

CHICAGO BOTANIC GARDEN

The Chicago Botanic Garden was opened in 1972 and has quickly found an active place in the gardening world. It has some twenty-six different gardens, and its excellent team of contemporary garden designers includes Michael Van Valkenburgh, Peter Morrow Meyer, Geoffrey L. Rausch, James van Sweden, and John Brookes.

CHICAGO BOTANIC GARDEN

CHICAGO, ILLINOIS

John Brookes designed a walled English garden, which in itself has six areas: a vista garden, cottage garden, pergola garden, daisy garden, courtyard garden, and checkerboard garden. Each represents a different contribution of English garden design over the years.

CHICAGO BOTANIC GARDEN
CHICAGO, ILLINOIS

Two beautiful bonsai, a *Bougainvillea glabra* in bloom and an *Ulmus parvifolia*, proudly represent the Chicago Botanic Garden's world-famous collection of bonsai in twenty styles and including more than forty different kinds of plants.

20

THE CLOISTERS
NEW YORK CITY

The Cloisters in Fort Tryon Park on the northern end of Manhattan, part of the medieval department of the Metropolitan Museum of Art, is not a copy of any one medieval structure but a collection of rooms and gardens that suggest the complexity of a large monastery. It houses a magnificent collection of medieval art; cloisters transported stone by stone from three different orders in France—Benedictine, Cistercian, and Carmelite—and architectural elements from Germany and Spain as well as France. It opened to the public in 1938 on land given by John D. Rockefeller, Jr., who also funded both its buildings and art. The Bonnefont Cloister from a Cistercian abbey southwest of Toulouse has a central wellhead, four quince trees, and raised beds protected from the wind by wattling. It has a very extensive plant collection, mostly herbal in nature and both medicinal and culinary.

THE CLOISTERS

NEW YORK CITY

Rescued from an abandoned monastery at the foot of Mount Canigou in the Pyrenees, the Cuxa Cloister is divided into four quadrants with a central fountain; within each section there is a flowering tree—a cornelian cherry, a crab apple, a hawthorn, and a pear.

THE CLOISTERS
NEW YORK CITY

The wellhead at the center of the Bonnefont Cloister comes from the Venetian region of Italy and deep rope marks in its rim suggest a long history of daily use. The garden includes a medlar tree, common in the Middle Ages but very rare in this country.

THE CLOISTERS
NEW YORK CITY

At the heart of most medieval cloisters is a source for water, and an octagonal fountain from the nearby monastery of Saint-Genis-les-Fontaines occupies the center of the Cuxa Cloister. A third cloister, the Trie, from a long-vanished Carmelite convent near Toulouse, has wild European flowers similar to those found in the Unicorn Tapestry. Under the able guidance of the head horticulturist, Susan Moody, the gardens are a living testament to medieval times.

THE CLOISTERS
NEW YORK CITY

Changing with the seasons, potted plants enliven the arcades surrounding the cloister garths. Some of the boldly carved capitals atop the columns are simple and geometric, others picture flowers or birds or animals, and still others, complicated human scenes.

THE COBB/STANWELL GARDEN

SPRINGS, NEW YORK

The Cobb/Stanwell bulb garden emerges with unstoppable enthusiasm each spring. This American cottage garden bursts with colors carefully chosen and arranged with hours of thought in the preceding autumn months. A system of trays for each bed is employed, and painstaking care is used to match color, height, and blooming times for the enormous number of bulb varieties planted each autumn.

THE COBB/STANWELL GARDEN

SPRINGS, NEW YORK

Regimentally planted rows would be anathema here—the excitement is about colors and how they work together in close groupings. Each year, new hybrids which have been developed and offered via catalogues are enthusiastically planted to try new colors. It really is a labor of love which is fulfilled each spring after the long winter.

27

THE COBB/STANWELL GARDEN

SPRINGS, NEW YORK

When the over 630 varieties of daffodils and over 70 varieties of tulips have finally bloomed and gone, another showing of iris is used to take the eye away from the earlier bulbs. At that time, the daffodils and tulips have their leaves tied together and are then interplanted in any spare inch of earth with annuals for a full summer garden.

CONSTANTIA
MONTECITO, CALIFORNIA

This South African Dutch Colonial house was landscaped by Lockwood De Forest, Jr. (1898–1949), shortly after the stock market crash of 1929. The commission was to create a landscape of some grandeur, appropriate to the South African house and yet relatively inexpensive to maintain. There had been a creek bed beside the house, which De Forest developed into a wide pool with a small pool placed in the foreground to exaggerate its length. The pools come close to the sides of the hedged garden, with a backdrop of tall trees. Between the forecourt and garden there is an elevated grass terrace with an opening to the pools. One must ascend to the terrace and then descend to the garden, which increases the garden's importance. Classical statuary, surrounded by topiaried eugenia, draws the eye to the end of the pool. Plants native to South Africa—Cape honeysuckle, bird of paradise, lily of the Nile, and Cape pittosporum blend and anchor the building. De Forest's father had been a painter of the Hudson River School, and he himself also started out as a painter.

CHATEAU DE COURANCES
COURANCES, FRANCE

The Chateau de Courances seems to catch the light that falls on it and turn it into a verdant magic potion. This is a classic French formal garden, an intimate Versailles. It dates back to the seventeenth century, but only parts of that survive now, primarily the moat around the chateau and the entrance avenue of plane trees. The Chateau's owner was guillotined during the French Revolution, and for a period of forty years the house and garden were abandoned. Before World War I, the garden was re-created in seventeenth-century style by the landscape architect Achille Duchêne (1866–1947), who also worked at Vaux le Vicomte and the water gardens at Blenheim Palace. Most of Courances's design is now attributed to him. The chateau has a lateral axis of a broad canal with plane trees overhanging its entire length.

2

CHATEAU DE COURANCES

COURANCES, FRANCE

The front of the house looks out over a scrolled topiary boxwood garden; then a canal lying in a sheet of grass continues the eye into the distant landscape. Adjacent to that axis, cut into the woods, are a set of falling terraced canals with lion statuary guarding each end. Swans grace the water and glide quietly over the green light.

3

CHATEAU DE COURANCES

COURANCES, FRANCE

Adjacent again from the terraced canals is a final level canal surrounded by grass, boxwood hedging, and a tall wall of linden trees. These canals interact in the most powerful way with the reflection off the still water and the trees rising into a living canyon.

4

OSCAR DE LA RENTA GARDEN
CONNECTICUT

White roses abound on the front terrace of Oscar de La Renta's house, with a sweeping country view behind. Russell Page said that a garden would always be competing with the view there, so he laid it out on the other side of the hill. De La Renta was born in the Dominican Republic, where tropical plants grow profusely, and he has always been devoted to gardens. The Connecticut one has allées of trees, intimate formal gardens, and a double perennial border that runs for hundreds of yards. It is constantly being developed, for De La Renta is always trying something new.

5

A DELAWARE GARDEN

DELAWARE

In the 1920s, the site of this garden was a combination of mills and industrial buildings, and the owners decided to create a Grecian ruin or a Renaissance Revival garden. They used bricks from the old buildings and new concrete forms that were made to appear old. If the workers made the work look too well finished, it was rejected. Huge saltpeter kettles were placed on brick columns, and Grecian statuary was placed around a temple whose mosaic floor was never completed. Tall columns, half finished, were cast in concrete to look ancient.

6

A DELAWARE GARDEN

DELAWARE

Heroic male figures stand amongst the rambling boxwood, with an orchestra of trees behind incuding cypress, dogwoods, and paulownias.

7

A DELAWARE GARDEN

DELAWARE

A couple of stone benches are placed in front of two statues partially overgrown with ivy, which stand as if looking down on a scene. The garden works as a Grecian ruin, like walking into a live folly—which is what it was meant to be.

THE DICKERSON GARDEN

The Dickerson garden has views over the Potomac River, with a gracefully sweeping hill. The simplicity of this dogwood garden is its strength. A curving driveway lined with native azaleas, with an understory of white dogwoods, forms a shimmering white cloud all down the drive in spring. A mixture of white cornus mixed with pink is enough to paint an exotic picture in the rolling landscape.

DINGLETON
NEW HAMPSHIRE

In 1904, high on a hill overlooking Mount Ascutney, Augusta and Emily Slade commissioned Charles Platt to build them a house and garden. A three-terraced garden runs alongside the house, with a single axis directly aligned with the peak.

DINGLETON

NEW HAMPSHIRE

A circular rose garden leads down to a deeply shaded path with a single bird bath, then on to an elaborate white Italianate pergola. The axis continues through an arch in the pergola over some box-hedged beds with a central circular pool, and then off to the landscape beyond.

11

DINGLETON
NEW HAMPSHIRE

Ellen Shipman worked with the planting in this garden originally, and although that has changed over the years, the basic palette of old lilacs, roses, and peonies from the turn of century still exists. Some of the beds are now grassed over, but a mixture of foxglove, spirea, astilbe, phlox, and delphinium add informal color to the strength of the white pergola. This remains a wonderful garden, its spaces relating to the house and all aligned to the extended landscape, exactly in the style for which Platt is famous.

12

THE MARCIA DONAHUE GARDEN

BERKELEY, CALIFORNIA

Berkeley still has the air of independent thinking so evident in the 1960s, and artist Marcia Donahue's garden takes it a step further. The first impression is of being overwhelmed with visual information: all around there are shapes and forms, color and shade. One is encapsulated, up close to strange plants like Australian grass tree, kiwi, passionflower, various grasses, ginger, colacasia, and flowering banana. Mixed in there are brightly colored cups and saucers held aloft on iron rods, painted stones, iron sculptures, a white column on which sits a naked lady split in two, and many stone carvings. It is hard to know how far the garden goes or where it finishes above one. But as time passes and one is able to absorb it all, the forms join together, the lines move in patterns, and one can see the artist's work clearly. Marcia Donahue uses the garden for inspiration in her art, which she then puts back into the garden. Its size is small, but there is so much in it to see that it takes time, as it should.

DOWNSIDE ABBEY

STRATON-ON-THE-FOSSE, ENGLAND

Downside Abbey, founded in 1814 by monks from Douai in France, is an extensive complex of monastery and boys school. Close to the abbey church is a small tree and shrub garden that leads to a series of orchards and former vegetable gardens. The orchards remain, but four vegetable gardens now lie fallow, surrounded by hundreds of yards of tall, well-pruned yew hedges. Still farther from the church the lane is lined with beeches, horse chestnuts, elms, oaks, pines, and London plane trees.

DOWNSIDE ABBEY
STRATON-ON-THE-FOSSE, ENGLAND

Below the tree canopy a large variety of shrubs and bushes borders the lane, and Queen Anne's lace abounds like powdered sugar stenciled on a cake. Many of the monasteries grew all their own food up to the 1980s, when second Vatican Council decisions concerning lay brothers reduced the able manpower. The monks grew such an extensive variety of flora because they could not travel outside the boundaries of the enclosure and thus brought as much within as they could.

DOWNSIDE ABBEY

STRATON-ON-THE-FOSSE, ENGLAND

This lane was one choice for walking prayers, and finally ended in mature woodland with a blanket of white allium throughout.

16

DUMBARTON OAKS
WASHINGTON, DISTRICT OF COLUMBIA

Mr. and Mrs. Robert Woods Bliss purchased the 53-acre property in 1920 and two years later hired Beatrix Farrand (1872–1959) to help them with the garden, an undertaking that lasted the rest of Farrand's life. The brief for Farrand was beauty, a sense of history, and interest in winter as well as summer. Another requirement, since they were part of the diplomatic community, was spaces for entertaining. Farrand made the utmost of the site, utilizing the steep hillside with views between the several gardens slowly progressing from formal to naturalistic. Here, the vista from the Rose Garden down to the Herbaceous Border and the Cutting and Kitchen Gardens, which offer a splendid display of peonies.

DUMBARTON OAKS

WASHINGTON, DISTRICT OF COLUMBIA

In what is called the Herbaceous Border, the limited number of perennials are mainly flowering shrubs. Most of the color is provided seasonally by tulips, then summer annuals, then chrysanthemums.

DUMBARTON OAKS

WASHINGTON, DISTRICT OF COLUMBIA

The Ellipse is bounded by an aerial hedge of tightly clipped American hornbeams 16 feet high and 15 feet wide, created by Alden Hopkins when the original boxwood oval had to be replaced in 1958. Farrand had foreseen the possibility, and in her *Plant Book for Dumbarton Oaks*, which she wrote in 1941 after the Blisses had donated the property to Harvard University, suggested a strict and simple replacement, perhaps a wall. Around the same time, the pool in the center was replaced by the antique Provençal fountain that is there today.

DUMBARTON OAKS
WASHINGTON, DISTRICT OF COLUMBIA

Ruth Havey, Beatrix Farrand's principal assistant, played a very active role in the creation of the gardens, designing many of the beautifully carved urns and sculptural ornaments. At Mrs. Bliss's request, Havey turned the no-longer-needed tennis court into a very decorative Pebble Garden, with an antique French fountain at its apex.

THE DUQUETTE GARDEN

Tony and Elizabeth Beegle Duquette bought their Beverly Hills property in 1949 and slowly added to it. Duquette, renowned for his Hollywood set designs, turned the steep, canyon-sided backyard into his own fantastic set. All the romance of Hollywood movies comes together as one pagoda looks over to another, joined by gangplanks and latticed stairs, staghorn ferns and baskets of spider plants hung everywhere, under a canopy of tall eucalyptus banked behind by the blue of Agave Americana. In the evening, each pagoda is lighted and Chinese lanterns soften the night.

21

THE GARRET ECKBO GARDEN

BERKELEY, CALIFORNIA

The Garret Eckbo garden is divided into small rooms with different levels, simple and functional. Close to the gate entryway there is a rough wooden sculpture leading to brick steps and an enclosed garden room. One wall is an amalgam of wood cut and shaped randomly in vertical forms, creating a textured sculptural element. A very simple garden table and chairs, a Japanese maple, ivy-covered walls, and a modern cut-stone jar complete the scene. A vivid green patch of swirling grass overlooks a small sunken cutting garden. A side stairwell leads up the side of the house to a balcony overlooking San Francisco Bay. Eckbo (1910–2000) trained at The University of California at Berkeley and at Harvard University, where he and his fellow students Dan Kiley and James Rose exhorted modern landscape design to concern itself with the social activities of twentieth-century life. Eckbo wrote extensively and went through many professional partnerships, culminating in Eckbo, Dean, Austin, and Williams (EDAW).

22

THE ELMS

NEWPORT, RHODE ISLAND

Built from 1898 through 1901 as the summer home of Mr. and Mrs. Edward Julius Berwind, The Elms has been a National Historic Landmark since 1996. The house itself was designed by Philadelphia architect Horace Trumbauer, who modeled it after the mid-eighteenth-century French Chateau d'Asnières. The Classical Revival gardens were completed from 1907–14 and contain many fine specimen trees as well as a lavish lower garden complete with marble pavilions, terraces, fountains, and sunken parterres. The gardens have recently been restored by the Preservation Society of Newport County and are a beautiful setting for the marble and bronze sculptures and the eighteenth-century carriage house. The strength of this garden is in its trees, which are a wonderful example of ornamental boundary planting.

23

EVERMAY

Evermay sits high on a hill in Georgetown, with views of the Washington Monument. The house, which dates from 1792, was built in the Federal style for Samuel Davidson by the architect Nicholas King. In 1923, the property came into the Belin family and considerable restoration and improvements were made to the garden. The forecourt has a captivating stone fountain by Swedish sculptor Carl Milles (1875–1955). Simple and pure in form, it has a commanding presence.

EVERMAY

The front of the house is framed with white wisteria and looks over a series of descending terraces with a round temple overlooking them all. To connect the descending levels, features like fountains are employed, which work when viewed from above or below. One white marble saucer is flanked by two obelisks and sits above a half-moon pool on the lower terrace level. It is dressed on either side with boxwood and ivy and highlighted with bulbs in the foreground. A Rabbat fountain, fashioned after a Moroccan garden, is beautifully appropriate in scale within a room created by American hollies.

EVERMAY

Another garden features a cherub statuary pool with flanking topiary and dogwoods. The gardens are well defined within themselves and curtained with over thirty-two species of mature trees filling the boundaries. Evermay is a beautifully laid-out garden, still meticulously cared for by Harry Lammot Belin.

EXBURY GARDENS

SOUTHAMPTON, ENGLAND

Exbury is synonymous with rhododendrons and azaleas in any plantsman's mind. The garden at Exbury was started early in the 1900s by Lionel de Rothschild, and covers some 200 acres of mature rhododendrons and azaleas, bordered by the Beaulieu River. With a team of 150 men working for ten years, the property was cleared and prepared to receive seeds from China, Assam, Upper Burma, and the Himalayas, which were then germinated and tended.

EXBURY GARDENS

SOUTHAMPTON, ENGLAND

The numbers of plants involved was formidable, with some million rhododendrons collected and over a thousand crossed to create hybrids. The garden is now continued by Sir Edmond de Rothschild and his sons, Nicholas and Lionel, and has three main areas, Home wood, Witchers wood, and Yard wood. Lakes and bridges give the garden form as it goes from one rhododendron to another. The garden also has an extensive collection of trees, notably North American conifers, Japanese acers, American magnolias, and oaks. William Jackson Bean, one time curator of Kew Gardens, helped with this collection, and it now provides shelter and room for the azaleas—like this Wilson mauve pink—to mature.

EXBURY GARDENS

One of the rhododendrons, Fortune FCC, blooms infrequently, a light yellow color with large dark green leaves, but when it does, the excitement is palpable. Exbury gardens are a legacy of Lionel de Rothschild's love for plants that keeps on growing.

FILOLI
WOODSIDE, CALIFORNIA

There is no grand approach to Filoli, with tantalizing vistas of the house to build excitement, but when you walk through the garden gate, it takes your breath away. The immediate impression is of exacting pruning, formal symmetry, shapes and shadows. Deep green double allées and pairs of large cylindrical Irish yews, *Taxis baccata* 'stricta,' mark the principal and cross axes. Then, as you move into the rooms of the garden, it loosens up with kaleidoscopic color—pinks and creams in the spring blossoms of the Walled Garden, interwoven lavenders, dark reds, and silvers in the Knot Garden. William Bowers Bourn II and his wife, Agnes, created Filoli between 1917 and 1922, making up its name from a favorite creed: "Fight for a just cause, love your fellow man, live a good life." Architect Willis Polk designed the house, Bruce Porter the gardens, and Isabella Worn the flower plantings. Its second owner, Lurline Matson Roth, continued the work with plant seeds collected from around the world. In fact, within the garden's walls, the only two native species are oaks.

FILOLI

Some of the individual gardens at Filoli were inspired by the Bourns' trips to Europe, like the Dutch Garden and especially the Chartres Cathedral Window Garden. In the latter, clipped boxwood hedges and yew cushions suggest the leading in a stained-glass window, with bright-hued annuals representing the glass. Rose trees supply the beds with rhythmic vertical accents.

FILOLI
WOODSIDE, CALIFORNIA

One path in the Chartres Garden is on a lateral axis that runs the length of the garden and extends inside the house as a corridor. Throughout Filoli, hedges of yew, laurel, beech, box, and holly abound, all tightly ordered. In the formal gardens, shape builds upon shape, rounded ball in front of lateral lines against cylinder upon cylinder, and as the shadows lengthen, the garden comes alive.

THE MARGERY FISH GARDENS

The Margery Fish Gardens at East Lambrook Manor are famous for their cottage garden style, about which she wrote extensively. First established in the 1940s, the gardens were developed throughout the 1950s and 1960s. An ongoing restoration led by head gardener Mark Stainer is in progress. He consults the gardening texts and slides that Margery Fish created for authentic replication, but accepts the garden as a living museum that continues to grow in her style but is not bound to the form in which she left it.

THE MARGERY FISH GARDENS

Fish was renowned for her brilliant ability to mix plants effectively in a contained space. She dedicated much of her life to saving the old-fashioned varieties of cottage plants, and her garden proudly included feverfew, teasel, sword lilies, wallflowers, Welsh poppies, pulmonaria, and cottage tulips.

THE MARGERY FISH GARDENS

SOUTH PETHERTON, ENGLAND

The garden centers on the seventeenth-century Cotswold building and its irregular stone pathways, creating the intimate cottage style. An extensive collection of hardy geraniums is cared for at the garden, and a nursery of Fish's plants makes them available to the public. Her many books and articles made her an admired garden writer and many of her books, including *Cottage Garden Flowers* and *We Made a Garden,* are still in print.

A FORT WORTH GARDEN

TEXAS

The straight lines of the modern house are reflected in the lines of the garden and join together in tight unison. The garden was designed by Russell Page (1906–1985) and has some of his favorite elements, like a defined central axis created by a pleached allée with a slate pathway running down the middle. Close to the house, which has a number of cantilevered elevations, a sunken reflecting pool emphasizes the changes in level; the lines are softened by hanging plants and the simple planting of white and colored violas.

A FORT WORTH GARDEN

A sunken rose garden is off to one side, with gray slate stonework on the paths and a large, shaded terrace. Between the roses and the terrace is a reflective lily pond flanked by a parterre garden. Agapanthus in pots softens the terrace and the whole garden is surrounded with tall juniper trees. The detailing is beautiful, with the levels between the rose garden and pool being joined by a squared boxwood hedge. It is an exceptional garden and is Page at his best.

RYAN GAINEY GARDEN

Ryan Gainey's flamboyant and colorful nature has been an engine in Southern gardening. Sharply observant and dynamically enthusiastic, Gainey has a love for flowers that is infectious. Searching for solid varieties of "old fashioned flowers" like salmon-colored Shirley poppies and single hollyhocks, he started collecting cuttings and seeds for his cottage garden. If plant combinations worked on a small scale, he would collect seed and then apply it on a larger scale the following year. His property was a nursery before he bought it, and included three greenhouses.

7

RYAN GAINEY GARDEN

DECATUR, GEORGIA

A terra-cotta urn with floral design is reflected in the surrounding plantings of daisies, lady's-mantle, and peony-flowered poppies and becomes the focal point in one of the garden beds. In the front of the house, flowers burst out of the garden almost onto the sidewalk, and it is obvious as you drive down the street that this is an exciting garden. A kitchen garden is planted with flowers intermingled with the vegetables. Everything he turns his hands to has to be beautiful—it is a standard he demands.

RYAN GAINEY GARDEN

DECATUR, GEORGIA

A white-flower arrangement that includes *Aruncus dioicus,* nicotiana, white foxgloves, and holly-hocks—all from the garden—shows Gainey's empathy with flowers. Starting with this cottage garden, Gainey went on to the retail business, garden design, event design, television, and books.

LINDA GARLAND ESTATE
BALI, INDONESIA

The Linda Garland estate has developed around an old *lumbung* or shepherd's house in the rice terraces of Bali. Garland, an extensively published interior designer and concerned environmentalist, has over eighty different kinds of bamboo on her property. The Balinese are very aware of the sense of place and also the alignment within a place, for example, whether something is facing the mountains or the sea. Both have strong symbolic importance, so how a house is placed, where a garden is situated, and even how one is aligned when sleeping, are critical.

LINDA GARLAND ESTATE
BALI, INDONESIA

With her design ideas, and using the artistic talents of the Balinese, the estate has developed into a wonderful spa retreat. A carved stone wall with moss growing over it gives a hint of the creative talent and innovative ideas employed.

GARUDA PARK

Take the simple idea of an interior garden open to the sky, with an octagonal structure around it that has no outer walls, set it down in a tropical forest beside a beach, and you begin to imagine Garuda Park. Landscape the surrounding forest with orchids, frangipani, hibiscus, and banana trees, and add the sound of the South Seas breaking on the nearby beach.

12

GARUDA PARK
BALI, INDONESIA

A beautiful dream wonderfully executed by two Englishmen, Harry Fane and Mark Shand, it was a retreat from their business lives in New York and London. Staghorn ferns, banana trees in pots, amaryllis, heliconias, crotons, and bougainvillea are part of the palette.

GARUDA PARK

The building and furniture are made from coconut palms and bamboo, the roof is woven of thatched ilang-ilang, which blends the house with the surroundings. Since the house is open all around, one always seems to be in the garden.

GIVERNY

CLOS NORMAND, FRANCE

Giverny, the garden and home of Claude Monet, was first begun in 1883, and has a profusion of flowerbeds, fruit trees, and ornamental trees. In front of the house the garden is about color and more color: roses, poppies, geraniums, and violas allowed to grow in a random manner. In 1893, Monet created a water garden across a small brook from the original property, and later added a pond inspired by Japanese gardens pictured in the Japanese prints he collected and admired. He painted the lily pond extensively, portraying the change of light and seasons. The Japanese bridge with wisteria climbing its roof provides a focal point, but for Monet, the garden's essence was the water lilies and the reflected surrounding trees.

SAMUEL GREEN GARDEN
CARTAGENA, COLOMBIA

The Samuel Green courtyard garden sits protected from the bustling city of Cartagena with the quiet splash of the fountain and an occasional shriek from the parrots. A small monkey jumps around in a black cage. Bougainvillea, ginger, birds of paradise, caladiums, anthuriums, and bromeliads overflow the flowerbeds. A hammock on the upper balcony is the perfect place to watch the plants grow when the heat of the day slows everything down. Cecil Beaton sketched that hammock in the visitor's book. It is the perfect place to give peace a chance.

16

C. Z. GUEST GARDEN
LONG ISLAND, NEW YORK

The bright-green gate of C. Z. Guest's garden room leads to three allées of mature trees that traverse the garden. Within the hedged garden room stand five tall topiaries topped with bird shapes. Russell Page found and placed these. The green of the gate is also used for a line of garden furniture Guest designed. Guest, who died in 2003, could also be said to have had a green pen, having written syndicated garden columns for more than twenty-five years. Her love for orchids is evident in a greenhouse full of them, from which she supplied the house with fresh color. There also are a vegetable garden, cutting garden, and a garden room with roses.

GWINN ESTATE

In 1905, William Gwinn Mather commissioned two prominent landscape architects to work with him on a new home. They were Warren H. Manning (1860–1938) and Charles Platt (1861–1933), an interesting choice as they came from different schools of design. Manning had worked for the Frederick Law Olmsted firm and was a proponent of irregular indigenous planting, whereas Platt championed the formal Italianate garden. They worked together surprisingly well, each eventually carving out areas to suit his own predilection. Ellen Biddle Shipman (1869–1950) was added to the team in 1914, when Mather found neither of the men sufficiently interested in planting the formal flower gardens. Twenty-one years later, in redesigning the formal garden for Mather and his wife, Shipman retained Platt's original organization, with its central pool and the copy of an Italian statue of Fortuna that he had commissioned from Tiffany and Company. But she softened its hard edges by adding flowering trees around the perimeter.

GWINN ESTATE

CLEVELAND, OHIO

Once the five-acre site on the shores of Lake Erie was chosen, Platt, who in addition to laying out the grounds designed the house, placed it close to the edge of a bluff thirty feet above the lake. He carved a series of broad curved terraces from the bluff and linked them to the house with flights of stairs. A pair of stone lions guards the bottom flight, which descends to the water.

THE THOMAS HALL GARDEN

BAR HARBOR, MAINE

The Thomas Hall Garden, set in woodland close by the Maine shore, has a very discreet green palette. Pathways in the mossy woodland of large conifers—among them American white cedars—are formed by bare earth and pine needles and lead to discreetly placed tall standing stones. Coming out of the woods, a sunken stone path picks its way through grass surrounded by mounds of mature ferns. A dogwood tree overhangs a small round pond and is understudied with moss and bunchberry. The simplicity of this garden is hauntingly beautiful.

THE HARLAND HAND GARDEN
SAN FRANCISCO, CALIFORNIA

To painter, plantsman, and garden designer Harland Hand (1922–1998), the garden was like a piece of fine art—something to be appreciated for its own sake. The half-acre hillside garden competes with the San Francisco Bay view, but there is so much going on at ground level that the view fades into the distant background.

21

THE HARLAND HAND GARDEN

SAN FRANCISCO, CALIFORNIA

Inspired by the color combinations of the High Sierras near Silver Lake, the light grays of granite, the dark greens of conifers, and the various colors of rock plants that grow in small cracks between ledges, Hand created beds, pools, rocks, and rounded steps with concrete forms. In and around these he planted yuccas, agaves, petite echeverias, aloes, angel's trumpets, treeferns, and *Magnolia grandiflora.* The combined colors and forms of succulents closely set together is the garden's hallmark. Hand did create a piece of fine art over forty years of work in his garden, which is now cared for by Marjory Harris, his friend and fellow plant collector.

22

THE MR. & MRS. HENRY HARRIS GARDEN
PHILADELPHIA, PENNSYLVANIA

The Harris's garden leans toward the Cotswolds, although it is firmly sited in Philadelphia. Old climbing roses hang off the walls behind myriads of delicate poppies intermingled with foxglove, delphinium, hollyhock, and campanula. The clean line of the gray slate lining the beds is softened by pinks, lobelia, soft violas, and lady's-mantle. No soil is left unadorned.

23

THE MR. & MRS. HENRY HARRIS GARDEN

PHILADELPHIA, PENNSYLVANIA

Into the mix go the heavier colors of 'Black Swan' tulips, 'Black Beauty' sweet William, black violas, and black fritillarias to bring forward the lighter colored poppies. Mrs. Harris is a painter, and the colors work beautifully together.

THE MR. & MRS. HENRY HARRIS GARDEN

PHILADELPHIA, PENNSYLVANIA

A simple knot garden sits perfectly on the terrace, with views toward the colorful flower border. Large weeping cherry trees overshadow the knot garden planted in boxwood and anchored in each corner with hydrangeas in terra-cotta pots.

THE MR. & MRS. HENRY HARRIS GARDEN

PHILADELPHIA, PENNSYLVANIA

Below the terrace is a half-moon seating area enclosed with boxwood, with views of a verdant valley off to the side of the house. It stands as a quiet contrast to the colorful border.

26

THE MR. & MRS. HENRY HARRIS GARDEN

BAR HARBOR, MAINE

The summer garden kept by the Harrises in Maine is close to the seashore. The strong summer light in Maine calls for a strong color palette. The blue of the sea and sky is matched with delphinium and highlighted with astilbe, rudbeckia, sedums, campanula, and alliums. To keep a tall border like this in good shape close to the sea, extensive staking is needed.

27

HATFIELD HOUSE

HATFIELD, ENGLAND

Robert Cecil built Hatfield House from 1607 to 1611 while he was Chief Minister to King James I. He had previously held the same post under Queen Elizabeth, and the Jacobean building footprint is in the shape of an E in her honor. The Elizabethan park and gardens were designed by Thomas Chandler, Saloman de Caux, and John Tradescant the Elder, who also collected plants from abroad. In the eighteenth century, when the landscape movement was in vogue, much of the Elizabethan gardens was lost. Then, starting in the mid-nineteenth century, the Cecils began to bring Jacobean elements back into the garden.

HATFIELD HOUSE
HATFIELD, ENGLAND

The house has always been in the Cecil family, and the Marquess and Marchioness of Salisbury have been very active in the restoration and re-creation of the gardens to their seventeenth-century character. Lady Salisbury designed a new knot garden in 1980, with many plants that Tradescant had originally used. It sits in front of the brick building in which Elizabeth I spent her childhood. South of the brick building or Old Palace is a scented garden which centers on a sundial and is surrounded by honeysuckles grown as standards and an extensive herb collection.

HATFIELD HOUSE
HATFIELD, ENGLAND

A large West Garden surrounded by pleached lime walks and inner yew hedges has a central fountain by Saloman de Caux. Its beds, cut into the grass, are filled with peonies, polemoniums, phlox, and dianthus. Robert Cecil had a fondness for dianthus, and Hatfield has a significant collection of more than 140 varieties. Farther from the house, there is extensive parkland with large mature trees.

HATFIELD HOUSE

Double avenues of standard evergreen Holm oaks, *Quercus ilex*, flank the East Garden. Its parterre of geometrically designed box-edged beds displays a mixture of roses and flowering perennials. Eighteenth-century Italian statues mark the ends of the cross-axis. Beyond lies a yew maze more than 150 years old. The Marchioness of Salisbury has brought the gardens back to full glory, relating them to both the house and the countryside.

HAY ESTATE

The Hay Estate goes back through three generations to John M. Hay, private secretary to Abraham Lincoln and later Secretary of State. The next generation, Clarence and Alice Appleton Hay, started significant gardening, and most recently there is nature writer John Hay. The house and garden are preserved under a combination of trusts and services, and the Garden Conservancy assists with the horticultural aspects.

2

HAY ESTATE
NEWBURY, NEW HAMPSHIRE

Clarence Hay planted a significant rock garden with some 600 rock and Alpine plants he collected. He kept accurate records on all the plants, including when and where they were collected, when and where planted, and how they fared. Using these comprehensive records, the garden has been restored with new varieties where old ones no longer survive. From the rock garden, a granite path winds its way down to a pond at the base of the hill set in the open landscape.

3

HAY ESTATE
NEWBURY, NEW HAMPSHIRE

In 1909, Alice created a perennial border in front of the house and, in what is now mostly wood-land, a shrub rose and perennial garden. This is called the Pan Garden, with some of the original azaleas, rhododendrons, and dogwoods remaining around beautiful dry-stone walls and urns. The two gardening styles are at different ends of the spectrum, but both left a beautiful legacy, which much skilled work is now restoring.

4

HERONSWOOD
KITSAP PENINSULA, WASHINGTON

The Heronswood Nursery catalogue is an invitation to immense gardening possibilities. Heronswood stands out as the preeminent nursery for introducing new plants from around the world and making them available to the gardening public. It is known for its delightfully quirky but very serious presentation of unusual perennials, shrubs, and trees. A border combination of phormium, bamboo, and geraniums—not an association often found—is a success because their striking differences make each plant show well.

HERONSWOOD
KITSAP PENINSULA, WASHINGTON

To visit the nursery and garden is to be confronted with the reality of all the Latin names—not as lists but as living plants—beautifully healthy and wonderfully laid out and cared for in a clearing of Douglas firs. Dan Hinkley and Robert Jones first came to this site in 1987, and initially continued to work full time as college lecturer and architect while the nursery was developing. The property is divided into two distinct parts, the nursery and their private house and garden. The garden is approached from the nursery through a wooden arbor down a long, double-sided ten-foot-deep perennial border packed from front to back. The variety of plants is staggering, some old favorites but many unfamiliar ones.

HERONSWOOD
KITSAP PENINSULA, WASHINGTON

The garden continues with a long, curving trellised arbor that leads to four quadrants around the house, each with a different color accent. The architectural structure of the house, paving, trellises, pools, arbors, benches, and fountains makes a good base for this plantsman's garden. Hinkley travels throughout the world to collect seed for propagation. In the woods there are other gardens with looser forms for trying out a plant's suitability, some with humorous sculptures, one with a pool and columns. The gardens around the house become very intimate and quiet, the spaces are tighter, and the plants have matured together.

HERONSWOOD
KITSAP PENINSULA, WASHINGTON

Often when walking in the garden, the fragrance of a plant can be as captivating as its form itself. There are gardens planted for blind people where the flower's fragrance and the touch of their leaves and stems are the determining factor. *Lilium formosanum* is a highly fragrant flower and would be a candidate in such a garden. It is also very beautiful, with striking red lines on its white flowers, and can hold its own in any border.

8

HIDCOTE MANOR GARDEN
GLOUCESTERSHIRE, ENGLAND

Hidcote Manor Garden was begun in 1907 by Major Lawrence Johnston (1871–1958), who was gifted as a plantsman and in spatial design, and was forty years in the making. This significant garden influenced many garden makers in the twentieth century, including Vita Sackville-West at Sissinghurst. It is noted for its garden rooms, which were created using extensive hedges of yew, holly, and beech, and also for its "mixed borders." In them, plant materials of different sorts were combined for an overall effect, as in the Red Border, where the trees, shrubs, perennials, annuals, and bulbs are carefully placed for their combined color effect. Hence, the color of copper beech leaves are as significant here as the blooms of the roses or poppies. This method of planting often involves semihardy plants, which require being housed in greenhouses over winter.

9

HIDCOTE MANOR GARDEN
GLOUCESTERSHIRE, ENGLAND

Johnston was born in Paris to a British mother and American father, and although the ideas in the garden are original to him, one can see the formality of the French garden as an underlying influence. A main axis terminates with the geometric shapes of pleached hornbeams creating two rectangles on either side of the path. A wrought-iron gate defines the garden boundary for this long axis with an appropriate formality. At other parts of the garden, a much softer delineation between the garden and the surrounding Cotswold countryside is achieved with loosely defined hedges, ferns, and wildflowers.

10

HIDCOTE MANOR GARDEN
GLOUCESTERSHIRE, ENGLAND

Johnston received plants constantly from other gardeners around the world, and in 1927 undertook a plant-collecting journey to Africa and China. Armed with this extensive plant palette, he laid out an intricate garden that flows from one room to another with many different aspects and ideas. The rooms have themes of color or shape and are experienced as distinct spaces. The hedges are often made up of different trees, creating a tapestry of colors within a unified shape. A small piece of statuary provides a focal point for the view across this circular pool between two leafed arches, and is unusual in a garden where most of the focal elements are topiary forms.

HIDCOTE MANOR GARDEN
GLOUCESTERSHIRE, ENGLAND

The garden as a whole also blends into the surrounding landscape almost seamlessly, at some points joining with cottages of the neighboring village. Taking the concept of borrowed landscape, the roofline of a nearby thatched cottage is echoed in the bones of this garden room.

HIDCOTE MANOR GARDEN

A simple tunnel of trained beech terminates with a bench. Johnston also developed a garden near Menton, in the South of France, where he grew his more tender plants. In 1948, he turned Hidcote over to the National Trust and retired to France. The garden is beautifully maintained, and any serious gardener should visit it.

THE HOMESTEAD
SHELTER ISLAND, NEW YORK

A tall privet hedge arching over a dark green gate gives little hint of the garden behind it. An abundance of *Rosa floribunda* 'Betty Prior' mixed with *Allium gigantium* greets one at the gate, skillfully dressing a swimming pool garden opposite a saltbox house built in 1791. A brick back porch holds pots of herbs and standard roses as well as dark green rocking chairs. A large, curved perennial border is backed by the tall privet hedge and fronted with a dry-stone wall that culminates in a grape-and-gourd arbor.

THE HOMESTEAD

SHELTER ISLAND, NEW YORK

From this arbor, vistas open up across a large pond to a second arbor on the hill. The bridge is not straight but angles in the center, reminiscent of Chinese and Japanese concepts that bridges should not be straight as protection against evil spirits; a bench provides seating above the water. From the arbor on the hill there are views to an obelisk, from that to a sculpture. The eye is pulled from one element to another by a path of laid slate slabs or just a swath cut in wildflowers. Plantings around the house, in the borders, by the pool, and in a cutting garden are full and graduated in shape and color. There is a lot of garden, all woven together not in separate rooms but as small parts of the whole.

THE HUMES STROLL GARDEN

Returning from Japan, Ambassador and Mrs. Humes set about creating a Japanese stroll garden. A garden of this style requires a deep understanding of Shintoism and Buddhism, and uses a convoluted symbolism of shapes, groupings, and arrangements. Its roots go as far back as Heian imperial design around 790. The Humes worked with a Japanese garden designer and his wife for four years, contending with a steep four-acre space. A Japanese stroll garden is concerned with the journey of one's mind rather than one's body. Aspects of the garden are symbolic of the natural world reduced in size. A small body of water may represent a lake.

THE HUMES STROLL GARDEN

MILL NECK, NEW YORK

Paths are never straight, nor is the eye ever drawn to focus on a single element. Dissimilar elements are arranged in triads representing heaven, man, and earth. Plantings tend to be evergreens, flowering plants being considered too transient. Trees like the Japanese maple are pruned down as a symbol of the reduction of nature. Set within these canons of design is the all-important tea-house or *cha-shitsu*, always placed with a view of the "lake." Recognizing its significance, the Garden Conservancy assumed care of the garden in 1993.

HUNNEWELL GARDEN

Standing majestically above Lake Waban is America's first Italianate garden. Horatio Hollis Hunnewell began to build his garden in the 1850s on a steep bluff below his house, after returning from fifteen years as a banker in Paris. He had visited many of the Italian-inspired gardens being built on English country estates, and decided to try out the topiary techniques they were reviving. His Italian garden leaped to instant fame when Henry Winthrop Sargent extolled it in his 1859 supplement to Andrew Jackson Downing's *Landscape Architecture.* Hunnewell created gardens in different styles in other parts of his property, as well as a pinetum in which he planned to grow all the pines that could survive the New England climate. He became an important benefactor of the Arnold Arboretum.

HUNNEWELL GARDEN

In the Italian garden, Hunnewell decided to see if American trees—native white pine, hemlock, and arborvitae—would take to topiary, which they did. Ironically, the traditional English yews he also planted did not do well, but he and his gardener managed to create better-acclimated hybrids by crossing them with Japanese yews. Some of the native white pines have been carefully pruned for 150 years.

HUNNEWELL GARDEN

WELLESLEY, MASSACHUSETTS

The Italian garden sits on seven terraces above the lake, and its topiaries are trimmed into a variety of shapes—cones, pyramids, and complex layered cylindrical forms. The shapes are aligned in an arc that follows the contours of the lake. The garden has been pruned by members of the Hunnewell family throughout the years, and is a real family legacy. When the sun rises over the lake and the shadows move round, the trees look like ballerinas standing tall.

HUNTERS HILL

NASHVILLE, TENNESSEE

The driveway curves upward and around until Hunters Hill is revealed—a stone house with a profusion of hedges and topiary laid out like an apron around it. The garden, created by Spook and Jamie Stream in collaboration with garden designer Ben Page, is striking in its use of shaped yew, boxwood, and barberry. Designing a garden to blend with the strength of the stone house called for strong lines and shapes.

HUNTERS HILL
NASHVILLE, TENNESSEE

Excellent stone paths close to the house keep changing either material or design; farther from the house, the paths become broad and grassed. Rustic wooden elements on a perimeter path include fencing topped with doves made by Ann Robinson, which leads to a wooden concave arbor. Peonies, ferns, and iris contrast with the regularity of the fence and boxwood squares. There are other plantings, like a massed rose arbor with vistas from the hill, tall grass, and extensive large boundary shrubs and trees.

HUNTERS HILL

Antique stone obelisks and benches, large terra-cotta jars, and a massive sculpture of a female face provide accents. But the garden's backbone is its interfolding shapes of boxwood and evergreens— green playing against green in squares, curves, pyramids, spheres, and running hedges.

HUNTINGTON BOTANICAL GARDENS

SAN MARINO, CALIFORNIA

In 1903, Henry Huntington bought the San Marino Ranch, which had splendid views of the San Gabriel Valley and the Sierra Madre, as the site for his Southern California home. Over the years, he and head horticulturist William Hertrich developed the estate, which opened to the public in 1927. Hertrich laid out the garden and collected plants, eventually becoming superintendent of the entire estate. The property now contains some 15,000 plant varieties arranged in a variety of gardens, laid out in a variety of styles. The broad lawn of the North Vista, looking to the mountains, is framed by allées of palm trees underplanted with camellias that show off Huntington's collection of Italian sculpture.

HUNTINGTON BOTANICAL GARDENS

SAN MARINO, CALIFORNIA

The Rose Garden has some 1,500 cultivars and is organized historically, so that the family of roses can be traced with actual specimens. Roses climb the long pergola that defines the northern and western sides of the garden, and, curling around arbors of wire hoops, overhang two of its paths.

HUNTINGTON BOTANICAL GARDENS

As a surprise for his wife, Huntington bought the Japanese Garden from a local teahouse that had gone out of business, transplanted it to a ravine on his property, then augmented it with plants and artifacts shipped directly from Japan. In the early years, a Japanese family was hired to live in the pavilion and tend it. The garden is especially beautiful in the spring, when flowering trees surround the moon bridge.

HUNTINGTON BOTANICAL GARDENS

SAN MARINO, CALIFORNIA

William Hertrich loved cactus, but it took some time before Huntington came to share his passion. Once his employer was interested, Hertrich traveled to Mexico and the Southwest to find specimens, and bought many from other collectors. Now the Desert Garden in its twelve acres displays more than 4,000 species of desert plants. Where possible, plants are grouped geographically, but aesthetic considerations and required growing conditions have always played a role in the layout of the collection, which does not pretend to be an actual desert. The Huntington Botanical Garden's extensive scientific programs include propagation of desert plants for other gardeners, to prevent plants being collected from the wild.

THE INGRAM GARDEN

The Ingram Garden in Charleston was designed by Robert Chestnut and fits the needs of Charleston life. A gray slate floor emphasizes the white flowers and the green foliage of the hedge and ivy. Single white camellias are trained to fan the wall; shade is provided by magnolias and palm trees. The pool creates a focal point and, because it is sunken, makes the garden feel larger. All is enclosed with a wall high enough for privacy but low enough to keep the daylight. The furniture cushions and the walls are in the same color range, so they blend together. This Charleston garden has room in which to move around and entertain.

INNISFREE GARDENS

William Butler Yeats's poem "The Lake Isle of Innisfree" was the inspiration for the garden Walter and Marion Beck started in 1930: "I will arise and go now, and go to Innisfree. And I shall have some peace there, for peace comes dropping slow." Equally important was Beck's love for Chinese landscape paintings. He coined the term "Chinese cup garden" to denote the individual spaces in a Chinese garden for which there is no term in Chinese. As in a painted landscape scroll, each space is self-contained, yet, as you leave it, blends into the next. These three-dimensional pictures can be of any size. Lester Collins (1914–1993), a landscape architect and a friend of the couple since the late 1930s, studied in Japan and China in the 1950s. He advised the Becks and took over the design and management of the gardens after their deaths, when it became the property of the Innisfree Foundation. He enlarged and rearranged the garden so that all its varied experiences— its streams and bridges, its rocks and fountains—draw one back to the central space with its forty-acre lake.

THE JEMISON GARDEN

The foothills of the Sangre de Cristo Mountains form the backdrop for the Jemison garden. A collection of Rocky Mountain wildflowers grows freely next to the dark pink of Richard Jemison's painting studio. The blending of the flowers into the middle distance gives the feeling of an endless garden. Santa Fe's evening light brings out the magic in the hills, and simple though this planting is, it makes a beautiful vista.

JONES WOOD GARDEN
NEW YORK CITY

This communal garden is a treasure hidden in the center of a Manhattan block with brown-stone houses enclosing it. Laid out in two slate terraces, each with its own fountain and oblong flowerbeds, the garden is a riot of color in the spring, when thousands of tulips bloom. In 1919, the architectural firm of Edward Hewitt and William Emerson renovated the garden and the houses to create this shared space. The bones are set with a line of hawthorns on each terrace, and shading is provided by American elm, linden, and ailanthus trees. Night lighting installed by Susan Murray evenly illuminates hydrangeas, hostas, and andromeda around the fountains at night.

KYKUIT

The word Kykuit means "lookout" in Dutch, and it is very appropriate for the Rockefeller estate, which commands views up and down the Hudson River. John D. Rockefeller completed the building of the house in 1913, and landscape architect William Welles Bosworth laid out the extensive gardens in Beaux-Arts style with terraces close to the house blending into rolling landscapes beyond and plantings directing the eye to exceptional vistas toward the river. Bosworth was influenced by Edith Wharton's book *Italian Villas and Their Gardens.*

KYKUIT

TARRYTOWN, NEW YORK

Fountains and classical figures adorn focal points, including a Temple of Venus that anchors a lateral axis from the house. The Inner Garden has a rill between two fountains, with a sculpture by Aristide Maillol of a bather putting up her hair. An Italianate teahouse anchors one end of this axis, in front of which is an intricate fountain with two facing swans and small dragon figures.

KYKUIT

TARRYTOWN, NEW YORK

All the workmanship and details are of the highest order, but Bosworth deliberately included rough rocks to keep a country flavor. A simple green garden features a marble sculpture of Cleopatra by Fredrick Roth with four female statues in attendance. Bosworth's Beaux-Arts orientation led him to incorporate much classical statuary into the garden. Governor Nelson Rockefeller expanded the art collection in 1963, and for sixteen years some 70 major pieces of twentieth-century sculpture were placed throughout the garden. Works by Calder, Moore, Picasso, Noguchi, and Maillol play a major role in the garden today.

3

KYKUIT

Every winter, the garden is put to bed with painstaking care. The shrubs are wrapped along with the fountains and the gardens, taking on a completely different persona. The shrubs in the semicircular rose garden look like bodyguards around the central fountain.

4

KYKUIT

TARRYTOWN, NEW YORK

In the main forecourt, the large marble Oceanus and the Three Rivers fountain, also wrapped, hold a commanding position with views down the Hudson River toward New York City.

THE ELIZABETH LAWRENCE GARDEN
CHARLOTTE, NORTH CAROLINA

Southern garden writer and landscape architect Elizabeth Lawrence (1904–1985) was admired by many for her books, *Little Bulbs: A Tale of Two Gardens* and *A Southern Garden.* She had two gardens—one in Charlotte, the other in Raleigh—and the J. C. Raulston Arboretum at North Carolina State University has a border dedicated to her, with flowers she had grown. The Charlotte garden was photographed some time after her death, and the picture shows a row of holly bushes pruned high running next to an old stone wall. The central bed had an assortment of daffodils, hellebores, and Chinese roses. Among other remaining elements were a circular pool, an old arbor, a birdbath, and a bust of the Madonna and Child on the far wall with ivy growing on it. It does not take long for gardens to disappear, but some plants will keep on going untended, like old roses by gravestones.

LINCOLN MEMORIAL GARDEN

SPRINGFIELD, ILLINOIS

This garden of 63 acres sloping gently to Lake Springfield is a living memorial to Abraham Lincoln, and to the genius of Jens Jensen. Prodded by the Springfield Civic Garden Association, the city, Lincoln's home, donated the land and in 1935 commissioned the great landscape architect

Jens Jensen to design it. In addition to his many estate gardens, he had redesigned Humboldt, Garfield, and Douglas Parks and created Columbus Park in the West Parks System of Chicago. His 1939 book, *The Siftings*, expressed his belief in indigenous plants and in the socially democratic use of natural resources. He placed his signature "council rings" within the naturalistic plantings at various vantage points—paved circles walled with stone at seating height intended for anything from marshmallow roasting to stargazing.

JUNE

7

LINCOLN MEMORIAL GARDEN

SPRINGFIELD, ILLINOIS

The plants Jensen chose were all indigenous to the states of Kentucky, Illinois, and Indiana, where Lincoln had lived: oak, maple, locust, hickory, redbud, service berry, sweet gum, ash, beech, cherry, cottonwood, flowering dogwood, and basswood. Many of these natives were not available from nurseries, so volunteers collected seeds and acorns, which were then planted with great ceremony under his direction by the Boy and Girl Scouts.

8

LOTUS CAFÉ

UBUD, BALI

In front of the Pura Taman Saraswati Temple in Ubud is a double pool filled with lotus plants. Opposite this stands the Lotus Café. The lotus is a symbol in many Eastern religions, and various parts of the plant have symbolic meaning. The lotus is used for daily meditative prayer. As the flower opens in the first of the sun's morning rays, it symbolizes the interdependence of love. The flower stands for faithfulness and the pod for fruitfulness of offspring. In Bali, the majority of people are Hindus and are likely to have at least three temples in their daily life. A flower and small offering are given as a daily ritual.

9

LOTUSLAND
MONTECITO, CALIFORNIA

In 1941, the opera singer Ganna Walska (1887–1984) bought a 37-acre property in Montecito that had been Kinton Stevens' nursery. There were mature tropical trees already on site, and Peter Reidel and Paul Thiene created Italianate gardens with Californian plant material for the Gavit family between 1916 and 1938. A house designed by George Washington Smith was also built in the 1920s. When Walska took over the property she initially intended it to be a retreat for Tibetan monks, but this soon changed as an interest in gardens developed. She named the property Lotusland after the lotus, which grew in one of the ponds, and because of its symbolism as a holy plant for some religions. She started by replanting the forecourt with a weeping *Euphorbia ingens* and masses of golden barrel cactus.

LOTUSLAND

Lockwood de Forest supplied drawings for the area close to the house, although it is uncertain how much of that was realized. As Walska's interest developed, she drew on several garden designers, including Ralph T. Stevens, William Paylen, Charles Glass, and Oswald da Ros. In the beds close to the house, she added euphorbias, succulents, bromeliads, and cacti, with an edging of agaves.

LOTUSLAND
MONTECITO, CALIFORNIA

An open gate with two columns and spheres flanked by large agaves heralds the start of the Blue Garden, its dirt pathway edged with chunks of green-glass slag from a bottling factory. Ralph Stevens designed the Blue Garden with huge Chilean wine palms and blue Atlas cedars rising above a sheet of blue fescue. He also worked on a large garden clock and an outdoor theater, later replanted by Isabelle Greene in 1988.

LOTUSLAND

MONTECITO, CALIFORNIA

Late afternoon light intensifies the blue of the fescue and all the gray-blue shades of the Australian conifers behind the wine palms and Mexican blue palms.

LOTUSLAND

Perhaps the most exotic of the Lotusland gardens is the Aloe Garden, a pool garden edged in large abalone shells and surrounded by over a hundred different South African aloes and desert plants. Walska created two fountains from giant clam shells, which stand in partnership with the giant aloes, grugru, and ponytail palms. In 1968, William Paylen designed an Australian tree fern garden accented with staghorn ferns. Lotusland has had time to mature, and all of these very original ideas from excellent designers come together with operatic force.

JARDINS DU LUXEMBOURG

PARIS, FRANCE

Paris has many public parks and squares with green trees, so that Parisians need not feel totally cut off from nature and the green roots of the countryside. The Jardins du Luxembourg serve this purpose very well. Marie de Medicis built the Palais Luxembourg with sixty acres of surrounding gardens in 1615–20, after the assassination of her husband, King Henry IV, in 1610. The grounds have been open to the public since the seventeenth century. A notable feature is the Medicis Fountain, erected in 1861, with a reflecting canal in front of it. There are also formal gravel paths, manicured lawns, allées of box-shaped trees, avenues of well-trimmed chestnut trees, potted orange and palm trees in box planters known as *caisses de Versailles*, and seasonal flowers maintained by a crew of eighty gardeners. There are hidden treasures as well—for example, the bee-keeping school and the Verger du Luxembourg, a 190-year-old hand-tended orchard where a thousand espaliered apple and pear trees of some 600 varieties still produce exquisite fruit.

15

LYNDHURST

The Gothic revival house at Lyndhurst was designed in 1838 by Alexander Jackson Davis for William Paulding, mayor of New York City. Lyndhurst overlooks the Hudson River and is adjacent to Sunnyside, Washington Irving's home. The second owner, George Merritt, employed the German master gardener Ferdinand Mangold (1825–1905) to address the grounds, and his work lasted for forty years—through the third owner, the financier Jay Gould, and his daughter Helen. Mangold introduced a Victorian landscape style called the "gardenesque style" by John Claudius Loudon, an influential English garden designer and writer, which incorporated beds in circular or arabesque shapes among the tree groupings. A circular rose garden was added, as well as a fernery and a very large, steel-framed conservatory, the first of its kind in the United States. Many specimen trees still survive. Lyndhurst is an excellent example of Victorian landscape design, which was concurrent with the art of the Hudson River School of painting, but very different in character.

MADOO

"My dove" or Madoo, as artist Robert Dash calls his garden, is a part of his creative genius and always on the cutting edge. On an original acre of land Dash has pushed the garden envelope since 1967. Things are constantly changing, being moved, painted a different color, or just thrown out. His respect for the freedom of a plant to grow may mean that other objects have to leave. A moveable bench is part of the summer studio courtyard, its curving armrests echoing the curve in a privet hedge behind. Running along the back of the studio are limbed-up Arctic willows underplanted with sweet woodruff, prostrate winter creeper, bugbane, and hellebores.

MADOO

The Madoo garden is now nearly two acres in all, with separate summer and winter studios. Dash migrates with the seasons. The garden has rooms, and different gardens, and walks, and bridges, and gazebos, and gates, and lookouts, and mirrors, and mounds, and pools, and every manner of path. It is a huge garden in a small space. Dash also designed the Chinese-style pavilion that sits on a bridge over a pond.

MADOO

SAGAPONACK, NEW YORK

Using ingenious pruning of common species of privet, Arctic willow, Russian olive, and black pine, Dash laid down the bones on a modest budget. The vegetable garden gates are adorned with red finials, distinctly transforming the ordinary into an eye-catcher. The colors that Dash utilizes in the painted elements are primary and could be influenced by flower colors close by. He is a contemporary artist, and color is inherent in his thinking—on the canvas or in the garden.

MADOO

Swamped in flowers, this open gazebo with candles and chairs is ideal for conversation on a warm summer evening. Many plants are grown from seed, and Dash's palette does not cast away any plant—even a weed—if it is in the right place. Color against color, form against form, whimsy against intellect, Madoo is a New York treasure.

MAGNOLIA GARDENS

CHARLESTON, SOUTH CAROLINA

Throughout the garden Banksia and Cherokee roses, Carolina jasmine, and wisteria swing from giant canopy trees—bald cypresses, magnolias, and live oaks. Today, plants that maintain a year-long season of bloom have been added to the original palette of spring flowers. Still, the epitome of the garden's romantic appeal is to be found in the old azaleas and ancient live oaks dripping with Spanish moss along the meandering paths beside the Ashley River, initially the main road to Magnolia Plantation.

MAGNOLIA GARDENS

CHARLESTON, SOUTH CAROLINA

One of the early Ashley River plantations, dating back to 1676, Magnolia Gardens has been in the Drayton family for thirteen generations. The oldest part of the garden is an allée of live oak trees approaching the front of the house, a remnant of the original formal gardens. These were only dimly traceable when the Reverend John Grimke Drayton inherited the estate in 1841. He had been told that he had to work in the open air if he wanted to regain his health, so he set about creating the present gardens in large part with his own hands. As he had been educated for the ministry in England and in New York, he was well aware of the fashion for picturesque gardens.

MAGNOLIA GARDENS

CHARLESTON, SOUTH CAROLINA

Taking advantage of no longer used rice ponds along the swampy margins of the river, Drayton made them into lakes. He planted native bald cypresses around them, which dyed the water black and turned the lakes into dark mirrors. Then he began collecting camellias and azaleas. He was particularly successful with the indica azaleas, which had been considered impossible to grow outside of a greenhouse. His grew to monster size.

MAGNOLIA GARDENS

CHARLESTON, SOUTH CAROLINA

The Long White Bridge, which spans Big Cypress Lake, has become an icon of southern garden design. In 1870 Drayton, his finances depleted by the Civil War, opened the garden to the paying public, and before long Baedeker listed it as an American attraction on the same level as Niagara Falls and the Grand Canyon.

THE RICHARD MARTIN GARDEN

The canyons that rise above Los Angeles create wonderful vistas but are full of challenges for any gardener. The gradient is severe, and the constant winds can dry out seedlings before they get established. Garden designer Nancy Goslee Power collaborated with Richard Martin to create a garden that uses drought-tolerant plants in large groupings that traverse the rounded hill. Paths zigzag the property as much to view the garden as to get from one point to another. The colors of the garden stay in the purple range, with four varieties of lavender, jacarandas, ceanothus, *Echium fastuosum*, and various aloes. Massed plantings of gray-green buffalo grass, proteas, lavender, and olive trees band the hillside. A packed-soil pathway lined with purple iris leads the eye to a sculptural Aloe Bainesii backed by the curves of the distant canyon. Foliage form and color draw more attention here than flower color.

THE PETER MAY GARDEN
CONNECTICUT

Overlooking the rolling Connecticut hills, this garden, one of several on Peter May's estate, was designed by Deborah Nevins. A pergola caps the sunken terrace, with views through to the countryside reminiscent of Sir Edwin Lutyens's design at Hestercombe, England. An end wall with a circular portal has baskets hanging from the wooden trellises. The garden, a cross-axial design centered on a sundial with four large and lavishly planted perennial beds, sits below a formal lawn and is a surprise hidden from the ground floor of the main house. There is a lake in the valley and a vegetable and flower garden beside an immaculately kept greenhouse. Woodland walks extend into the surroundings.

THE DOUGLAS MAYHEW GARDEN

CONNECTICUT

Nestled beside the Housatonic River, Douglas Mayhew's country house is a melting pot of creative ideas. Salvaged elements of columns, cut marble, and industrial metalwork are all pulled into service as the structural background for his planting palette of cycas, araucaria, cryptomeria, agave, decksonia, and melianthus. One of the focal points is a seating area in a templelike structure created from six cast-iron columns canopied by multiple gourd plants.

THE DOUGLAS MAYHEW GARDEN
CONNECTICUT

Another Mayhew favorite is the castor oil plant, which he uses in his mixed-perennial bed and in large banks by itself. There is a walkway with large anthuriums growing out of elevated terra-cotta pots. Mayhew's creative drive has him constantly moving things with an energy that seems to be reflected in the plants' growth. As one moves around the garden, theatrical scenes unfold, with different groupings of objects and plants sculpturally laid out. One original idea leads to another, maintaining a sense of excitement.

THE NANCY McCABE GARDEN
CONNECTICUT

Mounds of red and white *Rosa rugosa* hedge the road from Nancy McCabe's cottage. There is a sunken garden set apart from the house, with perennial borders on three sides and an opening on the far side into some informal planting. There is a small herb and vegetable garden between the back of the house and a large rock outcropping beside the kitchen door. Some espaliered fruit trees shield the rock, and a tall evergreen hedge encloses the rest of the garden. Two potted standard rosemary bushes stand as sentries at the start of a small brick path, with accents of rough-cut marble set into it on the diagonal. The beds are flanked with terra-cotta edgings, and pots of herbs and dianthus are lined with lavender and hold rows of vegetables in different stages of maturity. It is a classic cottage vegetable garden, functional, convenient, small, and beautiful. Nancy McCabe is a garden designer, and this little backdoor garden pulls together a host of good ideas.

PATTI McGEE GARDEN

The city of Charleston is renowned for its historic houses and gardens, characterized by their courtyard gardens and container plantings. The gardens are often enclosed by brick buildings, with little space and deep shade. The Patti McGee garden is an excellent example of how to make the most of such constraints. Landscape architects Hugh and Mary Palmer Dargan worked on circulation by removing some structures, making an opening in a wall, and building an arbor. Narrow raised beds were placed around the walls and extensive container plantings were employed.

PATTI McGEE GARDEN
CHARLESTON, SOUTH CAROLINA

With ivy clinging to the brick walls, and a riot of ferns, anthurium, caladiums, clivia, boxwood, foxgloves, lobelia, verbena, cuphera, larkspur, pansies, geranium, silver germander, and jasmine, the courtyard just envelops one in plants. It is a perfect place to entertain, and is often graced with chamber music performances during the Spoleto Festival.

1

MIDDLETON PLACE PLANTATION

The gardens at Middleton Place were begun in 1741 by Henry Middleton and belonged to his descendants until 1974, when a foundation was created to preserve the plantation. The garden design reflects the grand architectural style in vogue in the early part of the eighteenth-century and epitomized by André Le Nôtre, designer of Versailles. Using principles of rational order, geometry, and balance to organize garden elements with woods and water, the gardens were laid out on an axis aimed down a straight section of the Ashley River. From the river, the axis runs between the two butterfly-wing lakes, up the central terracing, through the central hall of the house and out to the front gates of the property. The garden is laid out with mathematical precision and emphasizes vistas and strategic viewpoints.

MIDDLETON PLACE PLANTATION

CHARLESTON, SOUTH CAROLINA

The artificial butterfly lakes and terraces, which took more than a decade to create, give the landscape a captivating form, especially when the sunlight casts long shadows on them. In spring, the hillside south of the rice pond blazes with azaleas; in summer, Kalmias, magnolias, crape myrtles, and roses bloom in abundance amid fine statuary in the formal gardens.

3

MONTECITO GARDEN
MONTECITO, CALIFORNIA

A wonderful collaboration between its owner and garden designer Isabelle Clara Greene, this garden beautifully points to the future for garden design in drought-prone areas. It was conceived during extreme drought conditions in Southern California in 1982, with an open sloping southern exposure and limited water supply. The clean white lines of the house are echoed by a Japanese restraint throughout the garden. A balcony broad enough to be called a terrace and to house beds of succulents wraps around the house and overlooks the hillside garden. Red bougainvillea falling from the balcony connects the two spaces with a dash of strong color.

4

MONTECITO GARDEN

MONTECITO, CALIFORNIA

An espaliered fig tree is anchored with lavender against the white house, helping to soften its starkness. Because so little water was available, Isabelle Greene used flat stones and beds of contrasting gravels in beige and blue-gray to suggest streams and pools. Only the small recycling sunken pool in the entry courtyard has real water.

MONTECITO GARDEN
MONTECITO, CALIFORNIA

Carefully crafted concrete retaining walls create a mosaic of terraces on the southern slope. Looking down from the balcony, the terraces look like a paddy field in the Orient, but Greene says that the field patterns you see from an airplane flying across the United States were an equally important inspiration. Most beds have mass plantings of drought-resistant plants like yucca, aloe, fountain grass, sedum, and dusty miller, although some have the colorful flowers the owner loves. This is possible because beds can be irrigated separately.

6

MONTGOMERY PLACE

ANNANDALE-ON-HUDSON, NEW YORK

Janet Livingstone Montgomery started Montgomery Place in 1804 by building a Federal-style house and starting a commercial nursery. Her successors, her brother Edward Livingston and his wife, Louise, employed the architect A. J. Davis to restyle the house. Andrew Jackson Downing (1815–1852) who owned a nursery in Newburgh, informally advised on the grounds and later designed a flower garden around the conservatory. Downing was the influential editor of *The Horticulturist*, a periodical that supported scientific farming and democratization of the landscape. The German landscape gardener Hans Jacob Ehers (1803–1858) was commissioned to plant an arboretum in the 1840s. The trees and woodland walks at Montgomery Place are part of the maturing of the naturalism that Downing loved. Today, vistas to the distant Catskills, with trees framing the Hudson River, are almost as they were in Downing's day.

MONTICELLO

Thomas Jefferson's home at Monticello was made up of about 5,000 acres of farms and cottage industries. His house, which he constantly redesigned and altered for fifty years, sits on the brow of the hill with views all around. After 1809, Jefferson's political career was slowing down and he spent most of the last seventeen years of his life at home. During this time he founded and designed the University of Virginia, but also spent much time on his garden—a lifelong interest. In 1807, he had laid out twenty oval flowerbeds to embellish the house and a walkway around the West Lawn. Each bed was planted with different flowers, some of the seed coming from nurseryman Bernard McMahon of Philadelphia, who was Jefferson's garden mentor. A large vegetable garden lying below the West Lawn held some 330 varieties of vegetables; two orchards held some 170 varieties of fruit trees. He also planted an arboretum on the other side of the West Lawn. All this took immense amounts of labor—there were about 80 slaves in the Monticello complex. The gardens became a laboratory for ornamental and useful plants from around the world, some of which Jefferson had collected in his own travels to France in 1784, and others from constant correspondence with gardeners in the New World and the Old.

8

MORTON/CORDELL

Set in the rolling hills of Marin County, this classic Californian mission-style house was built with contemporary industrial building materials by architects Tom Cordell and David Morton. A central courtyard with a reflecting pool, buildings on two sides, and connecting covered walkways makes up the simple design. A large rolling door on one side of the enclosure opens up to a vista of wild grasses coming right up to the house, with clumps of oak trees in the distance. Six mature olive trees grow within the enclosure, their silver foliage blending with corrugated wall material.

9

MORTON/CORDELL
MARIN COUNTY, CALIFORNIA

The garden, just planted at the time of photography, was comprised of thirteen row beds with blueberries, currants, grapes, peaches, and nectarines. A variety of herbs and roses were getting established. This simple complex is so well sited and thought out that one is always aware of the vast landscape around it and the open sky above.

MOTTISFONT ABBEY

ROMSEY, ENGLAND

Mottisfont Abbey is a twelfth-century Augustinian priory that was converted to a private house after the Dissolution. The Abbey is nestled by a tributary of the River Test, with sweeping lawns, a large collection of mature trees, and walled gardens. The spring or "font" from which its name was taken still bubbles forth. Norah Lindsay (1866–1948), a garden designer prolific in the 1930s, worked on a parterre garden. Sir Geoffrey Jellicoe put in an avenue of lime trees and an octagonal yew garden. Then, in 1972, Graham Stuart Thomas created a walled rose garden.

MOTTISFONT ABBEY

ROMSEY, ENGLAND

Graham Stuart Thomas, writer and garden designer, became garden advisor to the National Trust in 1974 and worked on many of the larger National Trust properties. The rose garden at Mottisfont is now the National Collection of Old Fashioned Roses, with more than 300 varieties. In one corner of the garden, the brick wall supports old climbing roses and hybrid tea roses fill the box-edged beds.

MOTTISFONT ABBEY

ROMSEY, ENGLAND

The garden has deep borders of roses with other perennials intermingled and edgings of lavender, pinks, lamb's-ears, and boxwood. Columnar junipers add a vertical element, and a simple circular pond with a fountain forms a central element. The setting is crowned by an old Great Plane tree thought to be the largest in England.

MOUNT STEWART HOUSE

NEWTONARDS, COUNTY DOWN, NORTHERN IRELAND

Mount Stewart, an eighteenth-century house and garden, was originally the home of the Londonderry family, who played a leading role in British social and political life in their day. The 78-acre garden was created by Lady Edith Londonderry in the 1920s, and is noted for rare and unusual plants. She received plants from different parts of the British Empire and was in communication with the plant collectors George Forrest, Frank Kingdon Ward, and Clarence Elliott. She also received advice and garden plans from Sir John Ross and Gertrude Jekyll. Her aim was to have as many unusual plants as she could, especially those with a tropical feeling, and Mount Stewart is noted for its exceptional collection of eucalyptus trees. A tree peony is backed by Monterey cypress trained in arches by an oval pool.

MOUNT STEWART HOUSE

Lady Londonderry also commissioned a local craftsman, Thomas Beattie, to execute sculpted animals in designs she created in 1925. Monkeys holding urns over their heads were placed on tall columns. For the dodo terrace, sculptures of the extinct bird were placed in two sets of pairs facing each other. The beds were edged with various evergreens and had a color scheme which changed from grays, whites, and blues to orange and scarlet.

MOUNT STEWART HOUSE

NEWTONARDS, COUNTY DOWN, NORTHERN IRELAND

Wisteria trained on arches creates a tunnel hanging over a carpet of pink London pride blossoms. The garden is extensive: Among its many different parts are a sunken azalea garden that Gertrude Jekyll helped to design and a Shamrock garden with a topiary of an Irish harp and a bear created out of yew.

MOUNT STEWART HOUSE
NEWTONARDS, COUNTY DOWN, NORTHERN IRELAND

Close by a large stand of eucalyptus trees are blue meconopsis, primula candelabra, and hostas—creating a beautiful color combination.

MOUNT STEWART HOUSE

NEWTONARDS, COUNTY DOWN, NORTHERN IRELAND

Overlooking the lake—first excavated in 1840—is a Temple of the Winds built in 1785 by the architect James Stuart as a private dining house. Lady Londonderry, with suggestions by Gertrude Jekyll, landscaped the lake's surrounding grounds. She used a variety of trees, including silver-stemmed birches and maples grouped for their autumn color. Close to the edge, gunnera, iris, calla lilies, and water lilies were planted. In 1955, the National Trust took over the property and meticulously maintains the collection of unusual plants, topiary, and statuary, all put together in a strikingly original manner.

NAUMKEAG

Naumkeag is what was called a "Berkshire Cottage" at the turn of the century, and sits high above a plain where the Housatonic River flows. The house was designed by Stanford White in 1884, with early landscape design by Nathan Barrett. This was developed from 1926 to 1956 by the significant collaboration of landscape architect Fletcher Steele (1885–1971) and owner Mabel Choate (1871–1958). Terraced gardens on the hilly site include the Afternoon Garden, Tree Peony Garden, Rose Garden, and Chinese Garden. One walk, farther from the house, culminates in the famous Blue Steps—a series of fountains backed by blue-painted cement, with flanking curved steps. The flowing lines of the white handrails play off the white birch-tree forest through which the steps descend.

NEW YORK BOTANICAL GARDEN

In the middle of the Bronx there are fifty acres of uncut woodland, one of the lesser-known areas of the New York Botanical Garden, an institution founded by Nathaniel Lord Britton in 1891. The botanic garden is fully comprehensive within its 250 acres, with many specialized gardens. Many garden designers have left their imprint there, including Beatrix Farrand, Ellen Biddle Shipman, Marian Coffin, Alice Recknagel Ireys, Penelope Hobhouse, Lynden B. Miller, Susan Child, and Patrick Chassé. It is also a major horticultural resource and center for plant-science research. The garden has an extensive botanic library, herbarium, and collection of live plants. The Enid A. Haupt Conservatory has climatic galleries for Palms of the Americas, Lowland Tropical Rainforest, Aquatic Plants and Vines, Upland Tropical Rainforest, Deserts of the Americas, Deserts of Africa, Hanging Baskets, and Carnivorous Plants. The conservatory also hosts special seasonal displays, which are very popular with the general public. Evergreen topiary trees in front of the main dome announce a winter exhibition.

NEW YORK BOTANICAL GARDEN

Inside the conservatory's long house, the exhibition Green Geometry features a vista alternating white benches with topiaries. These unbelievably precise geometric fantasies were created by Gary D. Barnum of Cooperstown, New York, who also designed the display.

NEW YORK BOTANICAL GARDEN

In a recent version of The Orchid Show, which takes place every year in late February and March, the reflecting pool under the main dome holds round planters packed with orchids. *Dontaenopsis* 'Minho Princess' offers a pink pyramid; *Phalaenopsis* 'Taisuco Swan,' a white one.

NEW YORK BOTANICAL GARDEN

THE BRONX, NEW YORK

More orchids—oncidiums, vandas, dendrobiums, and phalaenopsis among them—cling to the roof of The Plant Collector's House nestled among tropical rainforest plants in the same exhibition.

NEWTON GARDENS

One of the most innovative combinations of landscape, winery, and garden sits on Spring Mountain in the Napa Valley. All the production facilities of The Newton Vineyard are hidden in the vine-covered hills or under the gardens. The idea of hiding necessities is as old as landscape design, but the planning of this site is shocking and good. When Mr. Peter and Dr. Su Hua Newton acquired the 560-acre property in 1978 to start their vineyard, they saw opportunities few could have imagined. The Chinese gates at the foot of the property hint at what is to come. Climbing a winding road through fields of vines, one expects to see buildings, but they are nowhere; then a view down into a formal garden with parterres and a fountain flanked with spiraled junipers catches the eye.

NEWTON GARDENS

There are eleven gardens here, each using the borrowed landscape all around. The Chinese garden, which is enclosed with evergreens, has the traditional ridged sand and placed stones, which echo the lines of vines curving up distant hills. One striking garden has a pool with five slate steps surrounding it, down which a sheet of water constantly flows. The pool nestles among tall conifers, a steep hill terraced with trellised arbors decked with roses rising behind it. Where are the fermentation room and all the maturing cellars? Under the formal garden and inside the hill.

JULY

25

NORTH HILL

READSBORO, VERMONT

North Hill is intelligent and significant but maintains a personal American style. Zone four on a Vermont hillside means about 100 frost-free days. The writers and garden designers Joe Eck and Wayne Winterrowd are comfortable with the growing-time limitation because the winter gives them time to write, design, and travel. Their love of gardening runs deep, as does their knowledge of plants. A seating area placed beside the back lawn is surrounded with agapanthus in white and purple, as well as white and blue hyssops, anise, and alabaster plant *Dudleya virens*. A large mound of *Artemisia* 'Powis Castle' provides a silver anchor, so the colors remain cool but accentuated.

NORTH HILL

The garden keeps the feel of a homestead with longhorn cows, ducks, chickens, cats, et al., but Eck and Winterrowd's design awareness is irrepressible in all they turn to, and that keeps the garden on the cutting edge. A dry-stone wall that separates the garden from the nearby country road is the backdrop for variegated sedge.

NORTH HILL

A terrace garden beside the house offers a sheltered area where tender potted plants are placed in the summer months after overwintering in the greenhouse. *Berberis Thunbergii* 'Ruby Glow' lines up below the wooden window frames of a conservatory in the house, and the ends of the garden are formed with boxwood and junipers. The flagstone pathway is filled with mounds of dianthus.

NORTH HILL

There are many gardens: a low terraced perennial border garden; a peony and rose walk; a rock garden; a terrace off the house with potted plants; a heather garden; a shade garden; a wonderful vegetable garden surrounded by thousands of spring bulbs. At the bottom of the garden is a greenhouse fronted by a stone wall with many rock plants in it. Close by this, a rock garden rises up a hillside, anchored at the bottom by a weeping willow and a variety of evergreens. At the base is a small stream where sedges, rushes, primulas, and water hyacinths grow. Occasionally, potted plants are set down for a thorough watering.

NORTH HILL

READSBORO, VERMONT

The early morning dew is caught in spiders' webs on the vibrant green of *Picea glauca* and the light is caught by the blooming *Macleaya cordata*. There are over 5,000 plant species in this five-acre garden, and the story of the twenty years of its making is well worth a book—and no one could have written it as well as Eck and Winterrowd did in *A Year at North Hill*.

ABBAYE NÔTRE DAME
LE BEC-HELLOUIN, NORMANDY, FRANCE

Le Bec-Hellouin is a Norman village set in the quietly rolling hills of Normandy and is neighbor to the famous Abbaye Nôtre Dame, which was first founded in 1034. It has had strong connections to Canterbury in England for nearly a thousand years. There have been periods of closure, but since 1948 the monks have followed a Benedictine life here. Bec is made up of an assortment of buildings from the fourteenth to the eighteenth centuries and sits in a broad, rich valley with farmland and cows grazing up to its walls. The cutting garden is a functional space between fields and ancient walls.

ABBAYE NÔTRE DAME

LE BEC-HELLOUIN, NORMANDY, FRANCE

Flowers are constantly needed for adorning the altar and for placing beneath the statue of St. Mary in the cloister garth, as well as for the guesthouses and other common areas. The cloister garth at Bec dates from the seventeenth century and has all the classic elements associated with a monastic cloister. The green grass is divided into four parts by paths with a central water feature. The grass is symbolic of the healing power of the color green, and the central water is symbolic of the garden of Eden. The four parts are symbolic of the four books of the gospels.

THE O'BOYLE GARDEN
CONNECTICUT

The O'Boyle family's house and garden were designed by Charles Platt. The house is set on a hill-top with garden rooms to one side, a walled lawn in the front, and a rock-face with dry-stone stairs covered by an arbor of grapes and old roses. The garden is lovingly kept, and some of the many old roses must be the original planting. An Italianate terrace on the front of the house creates a lateral axis to a sunken garden with a small fountain. Two box-edged beds are filled to overflowing with coral-pink snapdragons. A second garden room intersects this main axis and is enclosed by old roses climbing over a stone-and-wood pergola. An urn is its central element, with white and pink planting around.

OLD WESTBURY GARDENS

OLD WESTBURY, NEW YORK

Built in 1906 by John Shaffer Phipps, Old Westbury was designed in the style of a classic English estate by George Crawley of London in collaboration with Grosvenor Atterbury, Alfred Bossom, and Edward Hinkle. Huge beech allées run to the front of the house and continue behind it, creating the major axis from which abundant lakes and garden rooms spring. Of note are a boxwood garden with a reflecting pool and a statue of Diana the Huntress in front of Corinthian colonnades backed by weeping beech trees; a sunken rose garden set out in seventeenth-century style with a twelve-sided stone sundial, and old and new varieties in beds bordered by Japanese holly; a thatched cottage complete with cottage garden and white picket fence. There are many fine statues in the garden, including a sundial of Atlas supporting the earth on his shoulders and two lion statues facing each other with mature rhododendrons behind them.

3

OLD WESTBURY GARDENS

OLD WESTBURY, NEW YORK

The walled flower garden is the jewel in the crown, with terraced gardens planted with large groupings of varieties together, inspired by Gertrude Jekyll. A descending stairway for the main axis cuts across a path with a double border with astilbe, salvia, heuchera, Lady's mantle, and lavender.

4

OLD WESTBURY GARDENS

OLD WESTBURY, NEW YORK

Anchoring the center of the garden is an Italianate fountain. Ironwork above the entry gates and stone detailing in the balustrades, stairs, and on the high brick walls create the intricate frame for the colorful planting scheme. A side path has a predominance of bearded iris and foxgloves, with columbines and astilbes. Roses are on the walls and in the center of the garden.

5

OLD WESTBURY GARDENS

OLD WESTBURY, NEW YORK

The bottom of the walled garden has a large pool that terminates the main axis. A central pavilion housing a female statue is flanked by a semicircular wisteria-clad pergola. Dark-blue iris skirting the pool emphasize the turquoise color of the pergola. Lotus and lilies complete the scene.

A PHILADELPHIA GARDEN

The rose garden is put to bed for the winter in this Philadelphia garden. The roses have been cut back and mulched, and all the leaves removed. An armillary sphere stands in the center of the box circle, a very appropriate choice for a circular garden, which needs a central anchor. The different bands on the sphere represent the sun's rotational path in reference to the equator or the tropics, often with an arrow placed at a specific angle to act as the gnomon casting a shadow on the bands. Important tools for early navigation at sea, armillary spheres now are often used as garden ornaments, and few are correctly aligned. The circle as a complete garden boundary is rarely used, simply because most of our property boundaries are drawn with straight lines, but it can be set down within a larger area—as it was here. Winter is a good time to assess the bones of a garden.

THE CHARLES PLATT GARDEN

CORNISH, NEW HAMPSHIRE

Charles Platt (1861–1933) was an etcher of distinction who studied in New York and Paris and was accepted into the Paris Salon and the Royal Society of Painter-Etchers in England at a relatively young age. While on the Continent, he fell in love with Italian Renaissance villas. Platt published *Italian Gardens* in 1894, a book that placed him at the forefront of an American revival of more formal gardens, where the house is sited to interrelate with the landscape. To exemplify his ideas, he built his own house in the Cornish artist colony in 1889 and laid out the garden with topsoil from Litchfield, Connecticut. He also designed gardens and houses for friends in the artist colony at that time, and slowly larger commissions for city and country residences developed. Ellen Biddle Shipman was part of the community and worked with him for a time before opening her own office in New York City and going on to a successful career.

THE CHARLES PLATT GARDEN

CORNISH, NEW HAMPSHIRE

Platt aligned his garden with the north-south sweep of the river valley, and favored cottage garden-style plantings such as lupine, iris, phlox, old roses, day lilies, sedum, peonies, and poppies. Hedges were used to line brick paths, and a lawn was overviewed from a portico off the house, with borders all around. Eleanor, Platt's wife, tended the garden primarily. The great hurricane of 1938 destroyed a large grove of pine trees, opening a view to Mount Ascutney from the house. House and garden are lovingly maintained by the next generation, Charles Platt and his wife, Joan.

THE JANE KERR PLATT GARDEN
PORTLAND, OREGON

John Platt bought an old orchard in 1937 and approached Jane Kerr to help him design a garden. Within a year they were married, and after the house was built and most of the orchard cleared, Mrs. Platt, an artist and a extremely knowledgeable gardener, started planting seedlings. The garden's two-and-a-half acres are now home to remarkable collections of trees, especially conifers, shrubs, and rock garden plants. They are so carefully arranged that the mature garden never seems crowded.

THE JANE KERR PLATT GARDEN

PORTLAND, OREGON

One of the first trees one sees on arriving is a *Cedrus atlantica glauca pendula* that totally encompasses the garage. In the center of the lawn, a beautiful vertical shaft is formed by a rare weeping redwood standing majestically alone. Behind it, the lawn is bordered by an assortment of dogwoods, pines, redwoods, stewartias, magnolias, maples, and junipers that offer an ever-changing variety of blues and greens.

THE JANE KERR PLATT GARDEN

PORTLAND, OREGON

In the rock garden, fastigiate junipers punctuate pathside plantings of rhododendrons, dwarf conifers, and special dwarf trees like Japanese red pygmy maple. In spring, the rock garden sports a carpet of bright spring bulbs. Later in the season ornamental grasses, alliums, and lilies put color at ground level.

THE NANCY POWER GARDEN
SANTA MONICA, CALIFORNIA

As one drives through the suburbs of Santa Monica, Nancy Goslee Power's garden stands out as it erupts onto the sidewalk, though within the house there is no view of the road and it feels like countryside. There are several rooms to this garden, which are as much a part of the house, and different rooms of the house have views or lead into the garden rooms. A front window of the house looks out to an enclosed cottage garden room with a small pool. To the side of the house is a courtyard with a simple pool, in classic Spanish Mission vernacular; abundant bougainvillea matches the terra-cotta tiled floor. Off the back of the house is an herb, vegetable, and cutting flower garden with a border of succulents. The plantings of artichokes, artemisia, rue, cabbage, sage, tarragon, chives, and arugula are highlighted by Bonica roses and irises; a small water trough provides a focal point. The garden rooms are as much a part of the living space as the interior ones, and become an extension of the house and its decoration.

THE PREWITT GARDEN

Beds and beds of Saunders hybrid peonies hybridized by A. P. Saunders stand alone amongst trees and lawns in Ashland, the Henry Clay estate. A memorial to Mrs. Richard Prewitt, who grew the peonies herself, it is a striking scene in spring. One of the most prized Saunders hybrids has a mysterious background. In 1926, a package of seeds arrived in America from the Paris seedsmen Vilmorin, Andrieux, et Cie marked *Ozieri alba*. Professor Saunders could get no further information about this unknown genus from the company, so he germinated the seeds and eventually created from them the beautiful white peony Halycon.

THE PRIORY

Peter and Elizabeth Healing moved to The Priory in 1938, and after the war spent twelve years designing the garden. There were already some old elements, like a 300-year-old yew mound that stands more than 25 feet high and is even broader at its circumference. They started creating garden rooms and put in some large herbaceous borders. The main focus of the garden is about color and how different colors work together. An intimate part of the garden is enclosed by a wall, and a neighboring thatched roof with two terraces, one below the other. Each terrace has a square pool, the upper one with a fountain and raised stone surround, the lower one sunken in grass. Each pool has a bench beside it, the upper one stone and the lower one wood. Silver and yellow plants impart a mellow feeling.

A GARDEN IN PROVENCE

FRANCE

Over the years, three designers—Peter Coates, Rosemary Verey, and Ryan Gainey—have worked on this garden in Provence. There is a small formal knot garden next to broad steps as you approach the front of the limestone house. A seating area shaded with a grape arbor, also at the front of the house, looks down a lawn to an allée of cypress leading to a swimming pool and a wildflower meadow. The late afternoon light casts vertical shadows across the lawn and highlights the stairs to the pool.

A GARDEN IN PROVENCE

FRANCE

A second seating area has views over a lavender field to a formal kitchen garden in the west and catches the evening light. An old stone table with dolphin-carved ends is shaded by a large tree and surrounded by rounded boxwood grown in terra-cotta pots. Lavender is grown as a crop in Provence for its oil and is cultivated in long rows that draw dark blue lines on the fields when it is blooming.

A GARDEN IN PROVENCE
FRANCE

Just below the dolphin stone table at the level of the lavender is a fountain with a semicircular pool. The pool is flanked on either side with light pink climbing roses and stands at the head of a mature rosemary-bush axis running down to a pair of enclosed potagers.

18

A GARDEN IN PROVENCE

FRANCE

Gray and green santolina and boxwood give structure to a circular design with beds of herbs and vegetables. Looking over one of the potagers across the field of lavender and rosemary bushes, one can appreciate the complexity of the tree planting in the upper garden.

19

LA PURISIMA MISSION STATE HISTORIC PARK

LOMPOC, CALIFORNIA

Twenty-one Jesuit missions, each a day's walk from the last, spread up the California coast from San Diego to Sonoma by the end of the eighteenth century. La Purisima, founded in 1787 as the Mission of the Immaculate Conception of Most Holy Mary, was number eleven in the chain. In 1812, it suffered a devastating earthquake and was moved to a more favorable location nearer to El Camino Real, the North-South travel route. The mission was a humble utilitarian building, some of its design features coming from the Andalusian Spanish influence, with enclosed courtyards and covered walkways beside the main buildings. The courtyards were used for bread making, brick baking, wine and olive oil pressing, and tanning hide.

20

LA PURISIMA MISSION STATE HISTORIC PARK

LOMPOC, CALIFORNIA

Fruits, vegetables, herbs, and flowers for the altar were grown in spaces called *huertas*, separated from the mission proper and often enclosed by hedges of opuntia like that in the photograph. Stock raising was a major source of income, and at one point La Purisima had some 20,000 livestock and 1,500 inhabitants. The missions were closed in 1834 by order of the Mexican government, but the Spanish courtyard design has lived on in the Californian vernacular. The California State Park system now oversees the restored mission.

LES QUATRE VENTS

LA MALBAIE, QUEBEC, CANADA

Mr. and Mrs. Frank Cabot's garden in Canada has similarities with their Stonecrop garden in New York State. Both sit high on hills with good vistas and have many gardens making up the whole. Les Quatre Vents is blessed with a feeling of being further from the bustle of life and more rural. The woodlands around the estate have many bridle paths that are alive with native *Cornus canadensis*, pink lady's-slipper, and caribou moss.

LES QUATRE VENTS

LA MALBAIE, QUEBEC, CANADA

Long allées of paper birch trees dissect the fields above the estate and intersect with equally long allées of Lombardy poplars that were planted on both sides of the driveway, with one set extending past the house and creating a wonderful tunnel approach to the house. These were the original bones of the garden, but their life span came to an end and they have recently been replaced with paper birches.

LES QUATRE VENTS

LA MALBAIE, QUEBEC, CANADA

One of the most significant aspects of this whole complex garden is Cabot's sculptural use of trees and hedges of thuja, hawthorn, and barberry to create rooms, forms, and allées. There are extensive shapings with thuja creating many distinctive rooms on the north side of the house. Each garden room is viewed from a room in the house—a bread garden where Mrs. Cabot bakes bread in an outdoor wood stove has topiary bread shapes and is visible from the kitchen window. A garden with topiary furnishing can be seen from a guest room. A little cup garden with a rustic fountain (*roche pleureuse*) is tucked away in a corner. This simple idea, beautifully executed, is typical of the hidden wonders of the garden.

LES QUATRE VENTS
LA MALBAIE, QUEBEC, CANADA

Frank Cabot utilizes all the indigenous landscape at his disposal, adding exciting ideas gleaned from visiting gardens around the world. The rope bridges are a good example of an entertaining way to see the ravine plantings of ligularia and petasites some twenty feet below—that is, if you have the nerve. To create a destination for those who braved the ravine, Cabot built the Pigeonnier and placed it within a complex of water gardens. Standing proudly at the end of a reflecting pool on one side and a small lake on the other, it is reminiscent of the Pin Mill at Bodnant in North Wales. The reflecting pool is flanked by thuja hedges on each side, which are in turn flanked by a double allée of small-leafed lindens under which primulas and bulbs are planted for a spring garden.

LES QUATRE VENTS

LA MALBAIE, QUEBEC, CANADA

Two authentic Japanese teahouses are placed at the end of the ravine with an appropriate "lake" and Japanese plantings. A woodland garden houses an extensive collection of primulas, which when they are blooming form wide belts of color along several small streams created for their irrigation. A terraced potager with wonderful delphiniums, often growing high over one's head, offers views down to the St. Lawrence River. There are also two serious perennial borders, a rose garden, a white garden, a meadow garden, a stream garden, and an herb knot garden.

LES QUATRE VENTS

LA MALBAIE, QUEBEC, CANADA

There is a small music pavilion, large enough for a string quartet to play in, near the top of the garden, and above that stands a Chinese moon bridge with its own small lake. A small road cuts across the garden between these two elements and looks down on a pool surrounded by *Petasites japonicus var. giganteus*, whose huge leaves create a rich green crater. Indeed, Les Quatre Vents is full of wonderful gardens, each beautiful in its own right. Cabot's book *The Greater Perfection* is a worthy tribute to them.

QUINTA DA BACALHÔA

SETUBAL, PORTUGAL

The son of Alfonso de Albuquerque, famous for pushing the Portuguese empire into India, was inspired by the art and gardens of Italy to build south of Lisbon between 1530 and 1550. His manor house combined Italian loggias with pepperpot towers reminiscent of Indian or Arabic architecture. The enclosed garden was to be viewed from the second-story loggia, where meals were served. Each bedroom also has a view onto the garden.

QUINTA DA BACALHÔA

Although its present scroll parterres show more recent eighteenth-century French influence, this is basically a classic early-Renaissance garden. Some subsequent owners took care of the house and gardens, still more neglected it, and by 1937 it was a pitiable ruin. Then it found an American savior, Mrs. Herbert Scoville, a woman of great taste and sensitivity, who painstakingly restored it using every available historic document.

29

QUINTA DA BACALHÔA

SETUBAL, PORTUGAL

At the opposite end of the garden from the manor house is a large *tanque*, a mirror of water, backed by a graceful, triple-towered pavilion. Such ornamental basins, which also serve as cisterns and holding tanks for irrigation, are a distinctive characteristic of Portuguese garden design. Today, they often are converted into swimming pools. A broad path runs between the parterre garden and basin alongside a sunken orchard.

QUINTA DA BACALHÔA

SETUBAL, PORTUGAL

Both house and garden were ornamented with what is now considered one of the most remarkable collections of Portuguese tiles or *azulejos* in existence. Some date back to the Renaissance, like those framing the bit of wall behind the tank. Others, like the blue diamonds on the stone bench, date from a later period. Tiles cover the interior walls of the pavilions and stone benches in the garden, and the loggia is home to five sixteenth-century polychrome tile pictures personifying the major rivers of Portugal.

QUINTA DA BACALHÔA
SETUBAL, PORTUGAL

On the outside of the path a wall of cypresses shields the garden from the road. Cut into the hedges below the trees at intervals are tiled seats, and some of these still retain their Renaissance pictorial tiles, one depicting the Rape of Europa.

RAGDALE
LAKE FOREST, ILLINOIS

Ragdale Prairie Garden—thirty acres of prairie grasses and wildflowers—has survived close to downtown Chicago since 1897 at the Arts and Crafts estate built by architect Howard Van Doren Shaw as his own residence. The estate has always been a haven for artists of all disciplines, continuing today as the Ragdale Foundation. Shaw had the foresight to encapsulate the property with a U-shaped path and allow trees to cover it like an English country lane. Behind the house is a formal garden with a dovecote in the same style; a small gate leads through a hedge into the prairie.

RAGDALE

Alice Ryerson, Shaw's granddaughter, identified 72 wildflowers growing there—including blue-stem turkey foot, a grass that the buffaloes ate. The prairie is burned off every year in March to prevent shrubs and trees from establishing. The grass and wildflowers move like waves of water when the wind blows. Colonies of particular flowers dominate in different areas each year, with the birds and insects singing praises all day long. Downtown seems a long way away.

3

RASHTRAPATI BHAVAN

The Rashtrapati Bhavan gardens were styled after Mughal gardens by the English architect Sir Edwin Lutyens (1869–1944) and represent a small part of the town plan he designed and completed for New Delhi. It is the presidential residence for India and was formerly the Viceroy's house. The gardens are laid out with intricately detailed pink sandstone hardscaping. There are terraces with canals and fountains, and *Mimusops Elengi* are trimmed to mimic the domed palace. This follows a particular Indian architectural vernacular called "Chatris"—in which umbrella-shaped roofs are repeated—which Lutyens brought into the plant material. He also used motifs of elephants and Indian temple bells on different elements, like gates and pillars.

4

RASHTRAPATI BHAVAN
NEW DELHI, INDIA

One of the motifs Lutyens deployed in the fountains at each intersection of the canals was that of the sacred lotus plant, which he did by layering sandstone circles as if they were leaves of the plant. As the water falls in the fountains and rills, it goes over stonework designed to create a particular pitch. Lutyens' genius for matching the spatial mass with intricate interconnecting details is beautifully retained.

5

RASHTRAPATI BHAVAN
NEW DELHI, INDIA

A circular garden with a central pond terminates the central axis. On each side of the axis, multiple rectangular beds are set into a larger matrix of rectangular canals with fountains at the canal intersections. The beds are planted with roses and annuals. The circular garden is enclosed with a tall wall and the beds descend in arced terraces. In 1931, when the gardens were completed, Delhi was a new city with very little indigenous vegetation, so what was planted here in broad color bands were the old faithful plants brought from England—like dahlias, calendulas, snapdragon, coreopsis, salvia, phlox, and poppies. At the end of each season, the best seeds were kept and replanted the next year with a change in location. However, the same plant material has been used since 1931. The pool is planted with lotus, which comes out later in the summer.

6

RASHTRAPATI BHAVAN
NEW DELHI, INDIA

Viewed from the top of the palace, the garden stretches out with symmetrical precision; then, turning to view in the opposite direction, the city of Delhi is similarly laid out. On one side all the business of government, on the other the country's premier garden.

7

THE MR. & MRS. WILLIAM T. RAYNER GARDEN

LONG ISLAND, NEW YORK

Mr. and Mrs. William T. Rayner's garden is still in its formative stages, fueled by the dynamic energy of their collaboration with Ryan Gainey. The garden has water views on two sides and a gradual, sloping terrain. There are terraces with potted plants, a long stone arbor with columnar yews interplanted with perennials, a grass walkway between hydrangea banks, and long-needle pines, a hedge-enclosed potager, a wooden walkway with banks of sweet peas, and a descending arched pathway with pinks, reds, and lavenders. A white rose garden enclosed with a yew hedge has jasmine growing on columns. The roses climb wooden obelisks within a boxwood parterre underplanted with *Stachys lantana:*

8

THE MR. & MRS. WILLIAM T. RAYNER GARDEN

LONG ISLAND, NEW YORK

At the end of the stone arbor is a fountain, and behind that a stand of *Acanthus balcanicus* are placed near a statue of a dog. The spires of the acanthus echo the limbed-up tree trunks behind them. The whole garden is exciting, refreshing, and packed with ideas.

THE DEAN RIDDLE GARDEN
CATSKILL MOUNTAINS, NEW YORK

The Dean Riddle garden, in the foothills of the Catskill Mountains, is proud of its Southern roots. Its 22-by-30-foot fence line was created in 1991 with cuttings of ash, oak, maple, and hickory. The formal plan has a center ball of *Petunia* 'Crimson Star,' with four oblong beds around it and four borders against each fence. The beds are edged with cobblestones and the pathways are trodden earth. Each of the beds has a mounded ball of box, *Buxus* 'Green Mound,' to anchor the corners. The back fence has some perennials and woody plants, which provide stability, and then each year different annuals are introduced. Volunteers like red orach, golden feverfew, corn poppies, and tall spikes of *Verbena bonariensis* are encouraged. Mixed in with the annuals are vegetables and herbs, all considered equally for their form and color. Most are replanted each year, so the color combinations are constantly changing but always beautiful. The garden receives constant attention and gives back tenfold.

JOHN AND MABLE RINGLING MUSEUM OF ART

SARASOTA, FLORIDA

The name Ringling is synonymous with the circus in America, and, if you are from Florida, with the state art museum. The John and Mable Ringling Museum of Art opened to the public in 1931 after the Ringlings had spent years collecting art, especially Italian Baroque paintings. The Venetian-style villa was designed by John H. Philips around a large, terraced courtyard. Surrounding three sides, a series of arches are supported by antique columns, and along the top stand statues of figures representing music, sculpture, architecture, and painting. Many early replica casts of major sculptures adorn the courtyard, with the Fountain of Oceanus and Fountain of Turtles overviewed by a large bronze David. There are twenty-eight enormous terra-cotta Italian oil jars, planted with bougainvillea, placed at intervals on the terrace. Tall palm trees provide a visual closing to the fourth side of the courtyard. A sunken pool area extends the interest, and a simple grass planting laid into the stone floor design gives the courtyard a soft, carpeted appearance.

11

ROCCHIA GARDEN
PORTLAND, OREGON

The Rocchia garden is informal, romantic, and creative. Set deep in evergreen forests beside a small river, it is full of lush growth. Andrew and Elizabeth Rocchia, a writer and watercolorist respectively, have created something of a cottage style, although it is really more relaxed and sophisticated. It is functional in its simplicity, with a grapevine of white Hungarian grapes that yield enough to produce a modest number of bottles each year; a very healthy herb garden; a bog area with hostas and white iris; and a wildflower garden next to the river. Old-fashioned plants like yellow loosestrife, daisies, evening primroses, California poppies, verbascum, digitalis, and hollyhocks abound. The garden has views cut out to the river or down a central path, but its main charm is the feeling of being gently surrounded by flowers.

12

ROSE COTTAGE
YORKSHIRE, ENGLAND

Gardening is second nature for many in England, who grow up with it as a normal part of life. Even a modest house in a city finds room to plant something of a garden. There are many cottage gardens throughout the country, and this Rose Cottage is a perfect example. The beauty of the cottage garden is that if a plant is happy somewhere, then let it grow. Color schemes are not labored. Flowers can be planted with vegetables and vegetables with flowers. Old varieties of plants are good enough indeed.

13

ROSE COTTAGE
YORKSHIRE, ENGLAND

The end result is a happy combination of peas and larkspur, runner beans and delphinium, onions and sedum, white and red roses, clematis and climbing roses. It is enough to stop a pedestrian in his tracks to hail the proud gardener with compliments. What better way is there to pass the time of day?

14

ROSEDOWN PLANTATION STATE HISTORIC SITE

ST. FRANCISVILLE, LOUISIANA

The main house at Rosedown Plantation was started in 1834 by Daniel Turnbull, and much of its nearly 3,500 acres was planted with cotton in very rich Mississippi Basin soil. In 1836, after they had traveled to gardens in France and Italy, his wife Martha started laying out a formal garden. A classic allée of live oaks runs up to the front of the house, and to one side is a formal flower garden with box-edged beds. Martha also ran a large vegetable garden to feed family and slaves, as well as an orchard, an herb garden, and a separate medical herb garden. Winding paths lead through two large tracts of woodland with white lattice summerhouses, fountains, and statues in clearings.

15

ROSEDOWN PLANTATION STATE HISTORIC SITE
ST. FRANCISVILLE, LOUISIANA

The plantation was kept intact through difficult times and is now a State historic site. Much of the original statuary is still in place, and large camellias and azaleas abound—possibly descended from the original plants purchased from William Prince & Son of New York in 1836.

SEPTEMBER

16

LA ROSERAIE DE L'HAY DU VAL DE MARNE
PARIS, FRANCE

La Rosaraie de l'Hay is a living museum of roses and the oldest garden devoted only to roses. It was started in 1894, when all the then-known species were collected by Jules Graveraux and grown here. Designed by the architect Eduard André as a formal garden, it now has some 15,000 bushes of 3,500 varieties. There are multiple rose beds with boxwood parterres, allées of rose trees, and rose-covered pillars, long walkways through arches of roses, and roses growing over trellises and temples. The main focal point is a trellised amphitheater and reflecting pool, with roses climbing all over it.

17

ROUSHAM PARK
OXFORDSHIRE, ENGLAND

The gardens at Rousham Park were designed in 1737 by William Kent (1684–1748). The owner of the modest 25-acre estate, General Dormer, called Kent in to work on a garden that had been designed by Charles Bridgeman (d.1738), who is credited with inventing the ha-ha. Kent came to designing gardens at the age of forty, after being a painter, architect, interior decorator, and furniture designer. Of the twelve gardens he created, Rousham was probably the smallest, but some thought it the best. Fortunately, it survives intact. Kent used screens of trees, statues, and buildings to define garden areas and create vistas into the surrounding landscape. The Cherwell flows beside the property, and Kent created a pavilion on a bluff above a loop of the river, with accented trees to pull one's eye into the landscape.

18

ROUSHAM PARK

OXFORDSHIRE, ENGLAND

Off the front of the house, an impeccable lawn leads the eye into a distant rural scene. A ha-ha allows the pastoral land to come close to the lawn; clumps of trees were planted or removed. Kent used what he called eye-catchers to anchor a view—like the Gothic triumphal arch behind which he introduced yew and other dark evergreens. He also designed benches and placed them at critical viewing points to the pastoral countryside.

ROUSHAM PARK
OXFORDSHIRE, ENGLAND

Closer to the house there is a large walled flower garden with old roses climbing on the wall and also extensively in mixed borders edged by boxwood, with repeating plantings of geraniums, iris, peony, artemisia, larkspur, and red valerian amongst the roses and other shrubs—like a large smoke tree.

20

ROUSHAM PARK

OXFORDSHIRE, ENGLAND

Behind the old carriage house is a rose garden with a large yew hedge and hybrid tea roses in boxwood-enclosed beds. Farther from the house there is a quiet garden where a rill runs through a verdant lawn, leading the eye to a lake with statuary focally placed. Rousham is a mature garden and encapsulates the English landscape garden.

21

ROYAL BOTANIC GARDENS

The Botanic Gardens at Peradeniya were established in 1821 on a site in a loop of the Mahaweli River, which had royal connections going back to the court of King Wickermabahu in 1371. The kings of Kandy resided here, and the grounds were already rich with plants when the British created a botanic garden for research to aid their various plantations. A sister botanic garden at Hakgala was also created—at 6,200 feet for research at a higher elevation than Peradeniya's 1,550 feet. Today, Peradeniya has a large number of very old trees, including three curving allées of palm trees, one each of *Borassus flabellifer* planted in, 1887, *Roystonea oleracea,* 1905, and *Roystonea regia,* 1950. Some of the trees form huge buttresses—like the Java Almond for example—that are in themselves sculptural forms. Some of the old formality of a botanic garden laid out by the British remains, with more recent plantings intertwined.

22

SAINT MARY-AT-LAMBETH

LONDON, ENGLAND

Next to the tomb of the two John Tradescants, elder and younger, is a knot garden beside the former Saint Mary church, which is now the Museum of Garden History. Fittingly, it was designed in the style of a seventeenth-century knot garden by Lady Salisbury, whose family in that period had commissioned the Tradescants to collect plants for their garden at Hatfield House. Saint Mary's only utilizes plants of the period, especially ones the Tradescants introduced to England. They were not only plant collectors, but were royal gardeners to Charles I and Charles II. The main structure of the garden is of interlacing varieties of boxwood with punctuated topiaries of myrtle, holly, bay, and viburnum. A spiraling, variegated Golden King holly secures the center. Interplanted in the various beds are shrubs and old plants like *Calendula officinalis, Digitalis purpurea, Nigella damascena,* iberis, and consolida. The Tradescants lived and had their own garden in Lambeth, not far from this site, which became a testing ground for the plants they brought back and became known as the "Ark," enough of a wonder in itself that people paid to visit.

23

SAINT PAUL'S WALDEN BURY

HERTFORDSHIRE, ENGLAND

The garden at St. Paul's Walden Bury is a fine example of early eighteenth-century classical design with an eighteenth-century house at its center. England's Queen Elizabeth the Queen Mother was born and spent part of her childhood at St. Paul's Walden Bury. The garden has beech hedge-lined avenues drawing the eye to beautiful vistas that focus on statues, temples, and the local village church tower. From the front of the main house, three axes fan out into the countryside, flanked on either side by stone statues of pairs of men locked in combat. Sir Geoffrey Jellicoe worked on several areas of the garden, including a glade named the "Running Footman Garden." The statue of a man in flight is sited in front of a reflecting pool opposite an elevated rotunda flanked with two sphinx statues, and is enclosed by the surrounding woodland and beech hedge.

24

SAINT PAUL'S WALDEN BURY
HERTFORDSHIRE, ENGLAND

There are many small gardens within the overall classical design, including an enclosed walled garden with statues of a young man in one corner and young lady on the other. Large terra-cotta urns sit upon the walls, and the garden is planted with old climbing roses, laburnum, and single yellow peonies.

25

SAINT PAUL'S WALDEN BURY

HERTFORDSHIRE, ENGLAND

One of the vistas leads down to a temple on the far side of a lake. The lake is hidden until one comes close, and then the temple is reflected in the water. Watching the sun move from behind a cloud and light up the long vistas as one walks down the verdant paths is breathtaking.

SAINT-PIERRE ABBAYE

SOLESMES, FRANCE

The gardens of Solesmes reflect not only the monastic needs of the Benedictine community, but also a strong association to French culture. Monastic roots go as far back as 1010 on this site, with many disruptions over the centuries. In 1831, a young monk named Dom Gueranger decided to recommence a Benedictine rule of life there and a new chapter opened. Now there are some twenty-one monasteries and eight convents around the world that have their roots in this community. The buildings at Solesmes were completed at different times and have a variety of gardens. There is a cloister garth with a fleur-de-lis scrolled in boxwood with geranium highlights. This is a reminder to the monks of their indigenous French culture.

27

SAINT-PIERRE ABBAYE

SOLESMES, FRANCE

There are informal guesthouse perennial gardens for people making retreats, and orchards and vegetable gardens where produce is grown in market-garden style. In the cloistered area of the monastery there is a formal French garden with topiaried yew in conical, box, and ball shapes. Set on a broad lawn with a double allée of linden trees creating cathedral-like spaces, it is a place for the monks to walk in prayer. The inner quadrants of the lawn are sunken, which accents the shadows formed by the yew shapes.

28

SANTA BARBARA BOTANIC GARDEN

SANTA BARBARA, CALIFORNIA

The Santa Barbara Botanic Garden had its beginnings in the Carnegie Institute and the Santa Barbara Museum of Natural History with a gift from Anna Dorinda Blaksley Bliss in 1927. A 65-acre property on a canyon rising high above the city of Santa Barbara was chosen for a botanic garden with an emphasis on the California Floristic Province. That year, some 2,800 trees and 2,000 bulbs were planted. The botanic garden is multifaceted, with a strong interest in the aesthetic as well as the educational and scientific applications of plants. The meadow garden was first planted with California poppies in 1940 and has a very naturalistic aesthetic. Plantings change through maturing and the meadow is no exception, but it retains an open spatial quality surrounded with canyon walls.

29

THE MARIA SCHNABEL GARDEN

LOS ANGELES, CALIFORNIA

The synthesis of modern architecture by Frank Gehry, Mediterranean planting by Nancy Power, and the intuitive eye of homeowner Maria Schnabel have produced an exciting, contemporary California garden. The sculptural shapes of Gehry's building are dressed with the punctuated forms of Brazilian cannas, birds of paradise, and agaves above carpeting of California poppies, sparaxis, and gray grasses. Black acacias and olive trees create a silver background from which the strong colors of the cannas jump out. Anchoring a corner of one building is a small grouping of three jelly palm trees, whose fronds are kept trimmed high. Their vertical strength and color mirrors bronze-colored shapes in an opposing building. The brown spikes of mature *Beschorneria yuccoides* stand out against the garden's white walls and add to the overall angular nature of the scene.

30

THE SEGAL GARDEN
LONG ISLAND, NEW YORK

The Segal garden was carved out of the flat Long Island landscape with a naturalistic swimming pool and a large pond. The pond is fed by a waterfall and lushly planted around with a variety of hostas, astilbe, iris, yellow musk, and ferns. The water itself is graced with water lilies and *Caltha palustris.* A perimeter path allows one to walk around the pond, but is kept narrow by the plant growth so as not to disturb the eye.

THE SEGAL GARDEN

The sun rises over the pond with a *Rodgersia sambucifolia* in the foreground. Several different varieties of hostas dominate the water edge, with yellow corydalis filling in the cracks.

2

THE SEGAL GARDEN
LONG ISLAND, NEW YORK

Creating an artificial pond takes extensive preparation, especially in porous soil, and often proves a never-ending undertaking. With a large pond, keeping the water circulating correctly and the pH reading nearly 7 is essential to prevent it being overgrown with green pond water algae or string algae. Once a good number of aquatic plants are established, it is more likely to stay stable. Water is difficult to manage in the garden in fountains and ponds and is prone to problems, but when it is working well, it can steal the show. Bearded iris are thriving around this clean water pond.

3

THE SEGAL GARDEN

LONG ISLAND, NEW YORK

A grass garden flanks the back of a nearby swimming pool with miscanthus, carex, and pennisetum, and is highlighted with large clumps of *Boltonia asteroides*. The pool is naturalized into the landscape with large boulders creating the edges and with a pathway, which in parts is subterranean with dry-stone walls. The walls and pool surround are planted with yuccas and rock plants.

4

THE SHANKS GARDEN

The Shanks garden is laid out with garden rooms connecting directly to the different sides of a modern house. Each has a garden room of different character, going from informal plantings on the south side to a formal garden on the east. The formal garden is best viewed from the house and has a small pond surrounded by beds radiating from it and with a central axial view. In summer it is planted as a white garden with hydrangeas, white irises, white water lilies, white valerian, *Chrysanthemum frutescens,* and *Lysimachia clethroides.* The beds are lined with boxwood, and a gradation of evergreens and deciduous trees creates a strong backdrop.

5

THE SHANKS GARDEN

This garden works well in winter, and by January in New York State any garden structure that holds the eye is a blessing. Winter changes values in a garden so much that even the permanent bricked surround, which provided visual structure in the summer, is lost under the snow. What becomes significant through the winter is what stands up and stays. So what was only a backdrop or hidden bones now becomes the main story.

6

SHUTE HOUSE
DORSET, ENGLAND

Shute House is an English garden where plants seem to love to grow. The three-acre garden is blessed with several springs, which enabled Sir Geoffrey Jellicoe (1900–1996), who redesigned the garden in 1970, to use one of his favorite elements, water. There is an enclosed canal garden with a bench under a mature rhododendron bush at one end. Under the bench, a spring gushes forth and feeds into the canal in one direction and into a rill that leads to descending flower gardens in the other. A long vista with an exaggerated perspective toward a female statue in the distance is bordered with iris, gunnera, and climbing roses. The stream falls over small chutes, each producing a different musical note as small bridges cross the stream.

7

SHUTE HOUSE

DORSET, ENGLAND

There is a topiary bedroom on the front of the house with a four-poster bed, an armchair, and a checkered grass-and-gravel carpet. Humor is constantly present in the garden, reflecting Lady Anne and Michael Tree's collaboration with Sir Geoffrey Jellicoe.

8

SHUTE HOUSE

Enclosed in the formality of large rectangular boxwood-edged beds, the flower garden allows the plants total freedom. The plants seem to love the environment and peonies, various geraniums, lady's mantle, poppies, and delphiniums thrive. Jellicoe was a founding member of the Institute of Landscape Architects, a writer, and a great thinker. He believed that the connection of the landscape to the subconscious is an unrecognized aspect of our contemporary lives.

A SOUTHAMPTON GARDEN

NEW YORK

This garden, within hearing distance of the Atlantic Ocean, was worked on by Mark Muskowitz and has several different garden areas. A deep grass border is planted on one side of the driveway, with side views through an orchard to the main house and a distant rock garden. An old shingle cottage, one of several outbuildings, has a colorful garden beside it planted with blues, silvers, pinks, and reds—poppies, peonies, lavender, catmint, astilbes, hostas, and climbing roses. The dark shingle sets off the color of the plants.

A SOUTHAMPTON GARDEN

A rock garden with curving lines and large boulders sits close to the swimming pool. The outer edges are planted with yuccas, grasses, carex, miscanthus, and phormiums, graduating up into larger shrubs. Sedum, cotyledons, and dwarf evergreens cling to the rocks. The garden works well in the autumn, with many berries in the background shrubs, and the grasses winter with interest.

11

A SOUTHAMPTON GARDEN

NEW YORK

A shaded fern garden opens to a raised crushed-shell pathway meandering through an iris garden. The beauty of this transitional garden, with its simple planting of blue and yellow iris highlighted with clumps of daisies, is its openness to the sky in the flat plains of the Hamptons. The sea can be heard crashing on the beach nearby.

12

CHINESE SCHOLAR'S GARDEN

STATEN ISLAND BOTANIC GARDEN, NEW YORK

The Chinese Scholar's Garden may seem a little hard-edged to the Western eye, but it is an authentic Suzhou garden. It was fourteen years in the planning, under the initial guidance of Gongwu Zou, a master restorer of Chinese historic gardens. The garden is only one acre in size but has three courts, a teahouse, three ponds, a waterfall, and five pavilions. There are no nails or metal in the building, which was created in China, shipped over, and meticulously reassembled by the craftsmen who had worked on it there. The elements of the garden are primarily symbolic: wood, rock, water, plants, walls, walkways, furniture, calligraphy, paintings, pavilions, and Xie— which is a building extending over the water. Some of the plants that China has given the world over the years are represented: roses, lilacs, daphnes, rhododendrons, and peonies.

13

THE SARA STEIN GARDEN

Garden writer and ecological advocate Sara Stein turned away from exotic nursery plants for her garden, using indigenous flora that many would call weeds. The garden is beautiful, and full of birds and wildlife. A few names on her plant list are yellow wood sorrel, Russian thistle, groundsel, arrowhead, sassafras, sage brush, dodder, jewelweed, ground ivy, evening primrose, Queen Anne's lace, fleabane, dandelion, Kentucky bluegrass—and, of course, goldenrod. Indeed, not much on her long list will be found in your local nursery.

14

THE SARA STEIN GARDEN

NEW YORK

Stein started with nursery plants, creating a conventional country garden with lawns and borders. As she displaced the wildflowers, she noticed there were fewer birds, butterflies, dragonflies, and ladybugs about.

15

THE SARA STEIN GARDEN
NEW YORK

The drift of wildflowers all blend together, with only a wild lily standing out. The algae on the pond have curved around, creating a line no gardener could have created.

THE SARA STEIN GARDEN

In the deep shade of a maple tree, a moss bank thrives beside the pond—Nature's natural lawn. Birdhouses are set up throughout the property to attract different birds, often with imaginative architecture like this church with steeple.

17

THE SARA STEIN GARDEN
NEW YORK

Blackeyed Susans, asters, and feverfew make up this drift with enough color and interest for any garden. Several years and books later, including *Noah's Garden* and *My Weeds,* one can see the country garden she set out to create, but with a radically different plant list. There are no hard edges, no jarring between plant materials—all works beautifully and is alive with birds.

18

STONECROP GARDENS

COLD SPRING, NEW YORK

Stonecrop is a pillar of contemporary American gardening, founded and supported by Mr. and Mrs. Frank Cabot. Cabot's love for rock plants and the excitement of collecting them in the mountainous areas of the world—from the Alps to the Szechuan Mountains of China—his many visits to English gardens, and an unstoppable vision helped him make Stonecrop an extraordinary garden. All this became a burden to Cabot, who also has his Canadian garden, Les Quatre Vents, and a new vision: to create an organization not unlike the English National Trust, but with the targeted responsibility of caring for significant American gardens after the death of their owners, the Garden Conservancy.

19

STONECROP GARDENS

COLD SPRING, NEW YORK

Caroline Burgess, an excellent gardener, began to take responsibility for Stonecrop Gardens. Gifted with vision, tenacity, encyclopedic plant knowledge, and taste, she has brought Stonecrop to new heights, especially in the use of semihardy perennials and annuals. The Inner Sanctum is a gray cedar-walled flower and vegetable garden where the plant color combinations are developed using this broad range of plant material. Cutting across the rectangular garden on the diagonal are several grassed paths creating island beds which are planted by flower color, graduating from reds and oranges to yellows and whites, then lavenders and blues. To create structure in these beds, wooden trellises give vertical height and have vines of golden hops, French beans, and morning glories growing up them.

20

STONECROP GARDENS

COLD SPRING, NEW YORK

A vegetable garden planted at the eastern end of the flower garden is watched over by a scarecrow fondly named "Miss Gertrude Jekyll." The full length of the flower garden and the extent of its planting can be seen from this vantage point. The wealth of plants is for the garden's educational function. Burgess's vision was to have Stonecrop become a school of horticulture, and with the Cabots' support the school has now passed its tenth year.

STONECROP GARDENS
COLD SPRING, NEW YORK

Stonecrop has an extensive collection of Alpine plants, which are housed in a meticulously kept Alpine house, as well as in raised beds, troughs, and a large rock ledge that stands above a lake with views to the Catskill Mountains. The normal habitat of Alpine plants is at high elevations, above the tree line. They tend to be small in size, but can be quite spectacular when they bloom in February and March.

STONECROP GARDENS

COLD SPRING, NEW YORK

Winter leaves behind the skeleton of the pleached and cordoned allée of small-leaved lindens around the flower garden. The tender and semihardy plants are all lifted by autumn and stored in a large, specially designed conservatory or in polytunnels. Through the winter, there is a display in the conservatory of South African, Australian, and New Zealand plants. There is always something in bloom in the garden, and a blackboard in the potting shed names each week's blooming plants.

23

STOURHEAD

Stourhead is a romantic landscape garden laid out by Henry Hoare II between 1741 and 1780. Hoare was a banker by trade, but he had a great talent for landscape design. Stourhead is unforgettable, the Romantic landscape garden personified. Set around a lake, the stroll garden presents incidents in Greek mythology as represented by a Temple of Apollo, a Temple of Flora, and a Pantheon designed by Henry Flitcroft (1697–1769). A Palladian bridge draws one into the garden circuit, and as one approaches, different prescribed views unfold both with the temples and across the lake into the distance.

STOURHEAD

STOURTON, ENGLAND

There is a beautiful sunken grotto with statues of a sleeping nymph at one end and an awakened Neptune at the other, both with cascading water from the river Stour. This is thought to be one of the earliest elements, constructed in the garden around 1740 with an opening on one side giving views across the lake. A huge tower known as Alfred's Folly is on an axis to the main house. Through the years, different plantings were added to the original design, with colorful rhododendrons and ornamental trees joining mature cedars, hemlocks, tulip trees, Chinese handkerchief trees, beeches, and oaks. The trees and their placement are the genius of the garden, the temples anchor the romance.

THE STRINGFELLOW GARDEN

The Stringfellow house was designed in the 1920s by John Byers, with a contemporary addition by Paul Lubowicki and Susan Lanier. The gardens were designed by Nancy Power. There is a small, walled front garden planted only with orange epidendrum orchids. It stands by itself as an additional room for the house, which opens to the back garden. There, large beds of lavender, *Lavandula multifida*, dominate the views. A slender, oblong water lily pool cuts into the overhanging lavender, extending the angular aspect of the house into the garden. Close to the house sits an informal stone terrace around an old pomegranate tree, which is enclosed by lavender. Around the walls there are plantings of echiums, geraniums, asters, euphorbias, and agaves. A large eucalyptus provides tall shade and completes the comfortable feeling of the garden.

26

A SUSSEX GARDEN

ENGLAND

Laid out by Sir Clough Williams-Ellis in the 1920s, this Sussex garden has an assortment of mature trees and great bones. Towering *Pinus sylvestris* and *Pinus radiata* straddle broad yew hedges enclosing a stream garden with a wisteria-clad stone pergola. The pergola terminates an axis, which goes through the tall yew hedge to the back of the main house. The two flanking pools are accented by terra-cotta urns with snow-in-summer and clumps of iris, sedge, and water lilies. Yellow fumitory quietly softens the front of the elegant building.

27

A SUSSEX GARDEN

ENGLAND

Different stone features are employed to emphasize the stream's course—bridges, dams, pools, and waterfalls. Passing the front of the pergola, the stream is flanked by tall columns of yew with ornamental trees and shrubs between: a pendulous beech, Japanese maples, and large rhododendrons.

A SUSSEX GARDEN

ENGLAND

The fertile soil—known as greensand—supports *Gunnera manicata*, *Primula florindae*, and *Hosta sieboldiana*. The garden is well protected and has a subtropical border with japonicas, yuccas, and fig trees. A variety of trees and mature shrubs gives this garden many different shapes and forms, with the yew hedge anchoring a central lateral line like the beat of a song.

THE TAVARES GARDEN
VILLA PANCHA, DOMINICAN REPUBLIC

The Tavares garden has been tended by the same family since it was begun in the 1930s by Dona Maria Grieser de Tavares and consequently continued by her three children. Extensive plant collecting throughout the tropics by the children led to a world class orchid collection growing alongside other exotic plants. Laid out around an old Dominican house with a central tiled courtyard, the garden has many rooms and walkways. The beds are laid out with curving forms and lined with a broad band of pebble edging. One notable garden room has ten-foot-tall, thirty-year-old *Vanda teres* orchids underplanted with pink impatiens.

THE TAVARES GARDEN
VILLA PANCHA, DOMINICAN REPUBLIC

A large descending fountain flows down a collection of old rum vats left over from a former family distillery. El Jardin Blanco, a white garden, follows the fountain, culminating in a covered pergola where jasmine, oxalis, euphorbias, and white impatiens are part of the plant palette. To one side, white thunbergia vine covers an outdoor eating area, which is blessed with the heavy scent of nearby gardenias and jasmine.

31

THE TAVARES GARDEN
VILLA PANCHA, DOMINICAN REPUBLIC

Tropical trees like Kapok and several varieties of mahogany provide high shade, and an especially large araucaria tree from Central America anchors one area. A big saman tree has chains hanging from its branches supporting large balls of staghorn ferns. There are native orchids growing from many trees and renantheras, oncidiums, cattleyas, arandas, vandas, arachnis, and ascocendas grow in mass plantings in the beds. The old trunks of tree ferns are used as supports for many of the orchids. A large grouping of orange epidendrum orchids greets visitors as they first enter the driveway.

CELIA THAXTER GARDEN

APPLEDORE ISLAND, NEW HAMPSHIRE

The poet and writer Celia Thaxter grew up on the Isles of Shoals, a bare and rocky archipelago some ten miles off the New Hampshire coast. Later, she lived on one of them, Appledore, with her husband during the summer months and gardened a small plot of land. The garden was ablaze with the colors of poppies, sweet peas, hollyhocks, nicotiana, lavender, larkspur, foxglove, and white rosa rugosa roses, and attracted painters such as Childe Hassam.

2

CELIA THAXTER GARDEN
APPLEDORE ISLAND, NEW HAMPSHIRE

Celia Thaxter's close observation and writing about the flowers and her absolute delight in them—particularly the poppies—have kept interest in her garden going. The Shoals Marine Laboratory on the island, a joint program of Cornell and the University of New Hampshire, restored the garden. Its staff helps many dedicated volunteers from the mainland to plant and water it each year.

3

THE THORNE/WOODHULL GARDEN

VERMONT

Anne Woodhull and Gordon Thorne's garden in the Vermont hills, has the feeling of a much-loved place. The vegetable and flower garden are set out in an open lawn some way from the house. A grass pathway leads through a maple sapling arch, with line after line of vegetables laid out on either side. Running parallel to the central path are two other grass paths, each accessing circular flower plantings—one path goes through pinks, silvers, and blues, the other through reds, yellows, purples, and oranges. The back of the garden is anchored with an old apple tree, tall sunflowers, and corn for the table. It is a beautiful working garden, the synthesis of two artists who keep their hands in the soil.

4

THUYA GARDEN

NORTHEAST HARBOR, MAINE

Thuya Garden was created by innkeeper and self-taught garden designer Charles Savage in an orchard at the summer lodge of Boston landscape architect Joseph Henry Curtis at the same time as he planted the Asticou Azalea Garden, both with the support of John D. Rockefeller, Jr. Both of these gardens were distant results of a disastrous fire that in 1947 destroyed a large part of Bar Harbor and devastated its tax base. Beatrix Jones Farrand, who had dreamed of turning her house and garden at Reef Point into an educational foundation, realized that sufficient support would be lacking. She decided to break up her plant collection rather than see it decline through lack of care. Savage took the opportunity of getting the plant material to plant both gardens. Thuya Garden is named after the predominant tree in the area, *Thuja occidentalis*, the American white cedar. A broad grass aisle is lined on each side with deep perennial borders that slowly change color. The lodge is now a library, and the garden has a tranquil, timeless air. The Island Foundation is a trust formed to care for the two gardens Savage created and eventually for the nearby garden Farrand had designed for John D. Rockefeller, Jr., and his wife, Abby Aldrich Rockefeller.

TINTINHULL HOUSE
SOMERSET, ENGLAND

Tintinhull House dates from the seventeenth century; its gardens were developed in various periods. There is an eighteenth-century garden off the front of the house, which is known as the Eagle Court Garden from the two eagle statues on tall columns that overlook it. This is a formal garden, its central stone pathway lined on either side with tightly trimmed boxwood mounds. In 1933, Captain and Mrs. Reiss acquired Tintinhull and put in a pool garden with a deep perennial border running alongside. One end of the pool is anchored by a stone teahouse and the other by an elevated antique urn; each corner has a large, planted terra-cotta pot.

TINTINHULL HOUSE
SOMERSET, ENGLAND

The axis created by the pathway in the Eagle Court passes over a circular pool with a white border, which terminates at a boxwood-enclosed white bench. A second axis starts from the circular pond into the vegetable garden lined with the purple of catmint and terminates in a farm gate and sheep-grazing field.

TINTINHULL HOUSE
SOMERSET, ENGLAND

An archway through the hedge of the kitchen garden gives views of the mixed border of the pool garden. *Crambe cordifolia* and verbascum provide a tall backdrop to the border on the other side of the yew hedge covered with glory vine.

TINTINHULL HOUSE
SOMERSET, ENGLAND

A kitchen garden intermingles plants with vegetables; here, huge old roses anchor the corners. The garden writer and designer Penelope Hobhouse lived and gardened at Tintinhull from 1980 to 1993, and her sophisticated color sense and plant combinations were beautifully exercised here at that time. It is now a National Trust property, and is focusing on the Reiss period in its maintenance.

9

A TOKYO PUBLIC GARDEN

JAPAN

There are five major parks in Tokyo created by decree in 1874. In one of them, Ueno Onshi Park, a pond is surrounded with green trees; yellow water lilies supply the only other color. Places of solitude like this in the packed city of Tokyo are rare and cherished. As Saint Hildegard of Bingen (1098–1179) noted, green has a healing power.

10

UPTON HOUSE

BANBURY, WARWICKSHIRE, ENGLAND

Upton House was built in 1695 for Sir Rushout Cullen and passed through the years without much interest until 1927, when Lord Bearsted bought the property. The gardens were developed in the 1930s, along with extensive interior renovations for his art collection. A new terrace was placed on the front of the house, leading onto an immaculate lawn. When one sits on the terrace, this lawn appears to be the extent of the garden—one must walk the length of the lawn before a large garden is revealed, running down the side of a valley with a formal lake at the bottom. On one side of the hill there is a sloping grass path with a perennial border on both sides that runs down to a large copper beech growing from the banks of the lake.

11

UPTON HOUSE
BANBURY, WARWICKSHIRE, ENGLAND

On the other side of the slope, an Italianate balustraded stone staircase connects a series of terraces that traverse the slope with a gentle hill rising up beyond. Red valerian and poppies paint a broad red splash on a cross terrace which is terminated by cedar trees. The garden holds the national collection of asters.

12

UPTON HOUSE
BANBURY, WARWICKSHIRE, ENGLAND

A large walled vegetable garden holds rows of vegetables and cutting flowers. Upton House has many gardens with a tremendous number of variations and intimate areas, but all share the common pastoral country view of the lake and fields beyond, often with sheep grazing. The house, art collection, and gardens were given to the National Trust in 1948 and are extremely well maintained.

13

THE MR. AND MRS. THOMAS VAIL GARDEN
HUNTING VALLEY, OHIO

Thomas V. H. Vail and his wife, Iris, turned a one-time stable into their home and named it L'Ecurie. With the help of two landscape architects, David H. Engel and Russell Page, the gardens became a work of genius. Page worked there between 1976 and 1983. He enclosed the front approach to the house with a pleached lime-tree surround, which gives an elevated green mass with vistas below. This technique, often used in Europe—he had worked in England, France, and Belgium—creates a solid oblong shadow, which adds interest to the eye. In the center of the front courtyard he placed a red maple tree. He also placed extensive plantings of white pine seedlings in the visible distant landscape to utilize the views through the lime-tree trunks under the foliage.

14

THE MR. AND MRS. THOMAS VAIL GARDEN

HUNTING VALLEY, OHIO

Behind the house, this pleached axis was continued with Washington hawthorns to screen a swimming pool. On the lateral axis, outside the library window, Page designed an intimate room shaded by Bradford pear trees with a central rill. A fountain at one end draws the eye down the rill into a miniature vista.

THE MR. AND MRS. THOMAS VAIL GARDEN

HUNTING VALLEY, OHIO

A gravel-covered floor completes the room. It is cool and inviting, clean and simple, clever and functional—the hallmarks of Page's work. The Vails developed a working relationship with Page that has led them to continue executing and maintaining the plans he drew up before his death in 1985.

16

VAL VERDE

MONTECITO, CALIFORNIA

Val Verde is a quintessential Californian garden of the great estates period. The original house and gardens, designed in 1915 by Bertrum Goodhue and landscape architect Charles Gibbs Adams for Henry Dater, had their roots in the Spanish Colonial Revival. After C. H. Ludington bought the estate in 1925 as a year-round residence, his son, Wright, and Lockwood De Forest began reworking the design of the house, the support buildings, and the landscape, adding some structures and simplifying others. Across the top of the slope, just below the house, De Forest created a 300-foot-long terrace. Beyond the house, the terrace walk is flanked on either side by rows of tall square columns that support neither elaborate capitals nor a pergola. They serve to anchor the house and create a strong lateral counterpoint to the line of stairs down to the ornamental pool which formed the main axis of Goodhue and Adams' garden.

17

VAL VERDE

MONTECITO, CALIFORNIA

De Forest simplified the planting on the descending hillside terraces. Cleanly cut box hedges reinforce their horizontal lines; carefully shaped mature oaks keep pulling the eye to the surrounding landscape. Throughout the gardens, architectural elements are punctuated by trees growing naturally but pruned to emphasize their structure.

VAL VERDE

De Forest used all the elements of the Italian Renaissance garden, but composed them in very modern ways. Fortunately, the Ludingtons, who were serious collectors, were clients who shared his tastes and appreciated the visual impact of his designs as well as their livability. He made a swimming pool and reflecting pools from no longer needed irrigation basins and integrated them seamlessly.

VAL VERDE

MONTECITO, CALIFORNIA

Originally there had been a rectangle of lawn at each end of the house. De Forest turned these into reflecting pools. While they balance each other, they are not identical in size or in treatment. The pool on the north side is surrounded by olive trees, the wider one on the south side is flanked by boxwood hedges and more columns.

VAL VERDE

Looking across the lotus urn in the south reflecting pool, glimpses of forest and mountains are framed by columns. Looking from the house, the urn is backed by a grove of oak trees that half hide a fountain jet. Water, dancing in fountains and mirroring the sky in placid pools, is the lifeblood of Val Verde.

21

VANDERBILT MANSION

HYDE PARK, NEW YORK

The estate in Hyde Park was bought by Frederick William Vanderbilt in 1895, more than fifty years after Andrew Jackson Downing had described the garden as "one of the finest specimens of the Romantic Style of Landscape gardening in America." Downing credited the design to André Parmentier, done while David Hosack owned the property in the 1820s. Vanderbilt promptly demolished the existing house and hired McKim, Mead & White to build a new one. From its semicircular portico facing the Hudson River, one can still appreciate the mature trees of Parmentier's naturalistic grounds and the view to the distant Catskill Mountains.

22

VANDERBILT MANSION

HYDE PARK, NEW YORK

In Vanderbilt's day, there were five greenhouses and twelve men responsible for the formal garden and grounds. The gardens have gone through several redesigns, and now, although the bones are still intact, no attempt is made to revive the high Victorian and very labor-intensive bedding out style in the formal gardens.

23

CHATEAU DE VERSAILLES

VERSAILLES, FRANCE

There is nowhere like Versailles, the ultimate French formal garden, which was laid out by André Le Nôtre (1613–1700) for Louis XIV after 1661. Versailles represents man's mastery over nature, the organization of nature's wildness with which man has had to contend throughout history. This was the Sun King's theater, made to impress and to express his grandeur. The site was swampy with irregular hillocks, a difficult starting point. But Le Nôtre was an architect as well as a gardener, botanist, and an avid collector of paintings. He and the team he led laid out the gardens with a main central axis down a Grand Canal centered on the palace. The king's demand for many grand fountains necessitated 120 miles of channels and underground aqueducts to bring pumped water from the Seine and Eure rivers. The volume of water required to run them all at once was too great, so engineers had the complicated task of turning on the fountains just as the king's party approached. To this day, the fountains are only turned on for specific periods.

CHATEAU DE VERSAILLES

VERSAILLES, FRANCE

The king wrote out specific instructions telling visitors how to perambulate the garden. *Le Bosquet de la Colonnade* was number twelve on Louis XIV's itinerary, and visitors were told to enjoy the fountains, the multicolored marble columns, the bas-reliefs, and the central statue, *The Abduction of Proserpine* by Girardon. Then, on leaving, they were to pause and admire a sculpture group by Guidi in which Fame holds up a portrait of the Sun King. According to Saint Simon, the colonnade had been finished by Mansart while Le Nôtre was in Italy, and on his return the king asked him what he thought of it. The response: "Sire, you have turned a mason into a gardener and he has given you his kind of handiwork."

CHATEAU DE VERSAILLES

VERSAILLES, FRANCE

The orangerie, the orange tree garden, and the *Lac de Suisses* merited three numbers, three to five, in the king's guide. The orangerie, tucked under the South Terrace where the orange and other tender trees in their boxes spent the winter, boasted the largest glass windows in the world at the time. From the terrace, the famous flights of a hundred steps led down on each side to the parterre where the orange trees were displayed in summer, with the large pool called the *Lac de Suisses* beyond.

VIZCAYA MUSEUM AND GARDENS

MIAMI, FLORIDA

The Italian Renaissance villa built by James Deering with wealth generated by the International Harvester Company was finished in 1916. He employed three designers—Paul Chalfin, Burrell Hoffman, and Diego Suarez—and nearly a third of Miami's work force to construct it. The formal gardens that surround it are a typical Beaux Arts blend of Italian, French, and Spanish ideas adjusted to the semitropical climate of southern Florida. What is very interesting is that Deering insisted on siting the house and gardens as close to Biscayne Bay as possible in order to preserve as much of the particular kind of native forest called a "hammock"—remarkable ecological sensitivity for that time. The most famous feature is the stone breakwater in the form of a ship opposite the east front of the house. Although far larger, it recalls the stone boats at Villa Lante in Italy and at the Palacio de Oca in Spain.

VIZCAYA MUSEUM AND GARDENS
MIAMI, FLORIDA

From the south facade of the house, the allées in formal gardens fan out in a typically French Baroque *patte-d'oie*. In the center, a green parterre punctuated with small topiaries of podocarpus is completely surrounded by a pool that is straight on the sides, curved at the ends, and studded with jets.

VIZCAYA MUSEUM AND GARDENS
MIAMI, FLORIDA

At the far end of the central parterre, a pair of grottoes with elaborately carved entrances flanks an Italianate water stair sloping down from a mount crowned by a casino or dining pavilion. Diego Suarez created the mount to block sun glare from the south-facing terrace of the house.

VIZCAYA MUSEUM AND GARDENS

MIAMI, FLORIDA

From the casino, flights of stairs shaded by live oaks and lined with carefully detailed rustic limestone descend on the east and west sides of the mount. The one on the east side leads to a circular rose garden, one of the many gardens hidden in the bosques around the main axis of the formal garden.

WATER RUN

HUDSON VALLEY, NEW YORK

Paul Mayen was inspired to create the gardens at Water Run in 1988. Mayen, designer and innovator, took classical ideas from formal gardens and twisted them just a bit into his own vernacular. He had connections to Fallingwater, the Frank Lloyd Wright masterwork, and in a play of words named his property Water Run. The garden has three unconnected major axes. The first runs between two facing pavilions at either end of an ever-green garden. A brown-gravel pathway lined with lavender runs directly from door to door of the pavilions. Shrubs graduated up to trees are accented by four classical stone sculptures. A small waterfall creates a central feature at the base of the shallow valley on which the pavilions face each other.

1

WATER RUN

Another axis starts at a triangular opening in a stone wall and leads to a broad path of upturned cement blocks highlighted with a white line created by white metal boxes. The axis carries the central white line through a circular white garden of white narcissus and peonies surrounded by a stone wall topped with white *Phlox subulata*.

2

WATER RUN

The white line continues up the hill, first delineated by white gravel and then by paint on the pathway with borders of Japanese iris forming bright lines of purple and blue with pink and red peonies behind.

3

WATER RUN

HUDSON VALLEY, NEW YORK

A third axial pathway is set between two stone pyramids with dry-stone walls on either side. An antique birdbath set on polished granite and surrounded by semicircles of arborvitae is a central feature. Mayen's use of stonework in pyramids, obelisks, walls, and pathways has created a strong structure for the garden.

WATER RUN

HUDSON VALLEY, NEW YORK

The obelisk at the end of the third axis becomes the center of a terminating garden. A blue bench sits in a splash of yellow achillea, with peonies, daisies, and iris. The obelisk has a man's face on two sides; on the one facing down the axis, the nose has been deliberately removed; on the other, facing a marble bench, the face wears a Grecian helmet with small wings. There are many rooms in this garden, where unusual sculptural elements demand more than a surface visit. In fact, Mayen intended that people look at it again and again.

5

THE WAUGH GARDEN

The Waugh residence has a variety of terrace gardens, with a pool area and a croquet lawn. Around the older part of the house, a higher terrace has palm trees with orchids on their trunks. Bougainvillea climbs over the building, and ferns, hibiscus, frangipani, ginger, and giant Swiss cheese plant are part of the palette.

6

WAVE HILL

Wave Hill commands views across the Hudson to the unspoiled west bank of the river. The estate's history dates back to 1843 but its present form dates from its acquisition by financier George W. Perkins in 1903. Perkins not only added several adjacent properties, he also reshaped the land, grading and adding new terracing, many rare trees, a subterranean swimming pool, a new greenhouse, and a variety of gardens. He was an active participant in creating the Palisades Interstate Park, which secured the protection of the view across the river. His descendents gave Wave Hill to the City of New York in 1960, but despite its public ownership, it still feels like a private estate. Even in winter, it offers plenty of horticultural interest to enrich its magical views.

7

WAVE HILL

THE BRONX, NEW YORK

Colorful flowers fill the conservatory all year long. It is now named for the recently retired director of horticulture, Marco Polo Stufano, who, beginning 1967, rejuvenated the gardens and turned Wave Hill into a mecca for plant lovers and gardeners. Beyond the conservatory door is the walled flower garden, a mixture of beloved old-fashioned perennials and interesting new cultivars. Careful planning ensures that enough berries, seedpods, and dried grasses remain to give winter interest.

8

WAVE HILL
THE BRONX, NEW YORK

Leaf color and texture are as important as flower color in all the gardens at Wave Hill, not just the flower garden but also the wild garden, the herb garden, the monocot (plants that have one seedleaf or cotyledon) garden, and the aquatic garden. This detail of the flower garden demonstrates Stufano's skill in combining textures and colors.

WAVE HILL

The flower garden's basic structure is critical to its year-round success. The rustic fence and benches, brick and stone paths, and clipped evergreen cushions are the bones of this typical Colonial Revival layout, and they survive the seasons. Tender plants that give height or spots of color live in pots and can retire to shelter.

WAVE HILL

THE BRONX, NEW YORK

The wild garden occupies a steep hillside behind the conservatory and palm house. Here, wild does not mean exclusively native plants. Rather it follows the concepts of English gardener William Robinson (1838–1935), who believed in allowing nature to take a hand in the composition by killing any plants, native or exotic—and he used both—that were unsuited to the place where they were planted.

11

WAVE HILL
THE BRONX, NEW YORK

At the top of the wild garden there is a U-shaped rustic pergola enclosing a sunken lawn, centered by a large formal pool planted with water lilies, papyrus, and bog iris among other aquatic plants. The mix changes from year to year, as it does in the monocot garden at one end of the space, home to grasses, bamboos, and lilies.

12

WEBSTER GARDEN

Set on a steep hillside, a lateral terrace stretching out from the Webster house is held fast by a retaining wall. The terrace is grassed, with three oblong sunken beds of vinca minor edged with ivy, the center one adjacent to the main axis. This is flanked on either side with three bands of white azaleas punctuated by balls of boxwood. Overhead, the white of flowering dogwoods fills the sky. As the sun moves around, the vinca changes from dark green to a sheet of light reflecting off its glossy leaves. Similarly, as the light moves around, the dogwood changes from almost invisible to brilliant white.

13

WESTERN HILLS NURSERY

Set deep in the redwoods of Northern California, Western Hills Nursery was started in 1960 by Lester Hawkins and Marshal Olbrich in a return to nature from an urban life in San Francisco. Self-taught through early planting errors, they introduced Mediterranean and Australian plants well suited to Northern California. Surrounded by tall redwoods, the plants can have either deep shade or strong sun. Paths meander through the plants, with a bridge here and there over a stream course, but this garden is not about structures or vistas, but about the plants. The nursery is now in the able hands of Maggie Wych, who continues the world-renowned tradition of healthy plants on the slopes of Western Hills.

14

THE MICHAEL WHITE GARDEN
UBUD, BALI

The Michael White garden, set on the side of a valley overlooking terraces of rice paddies and a rushing river, is full of exotic plants. An assortment of colorful foliage and flowers including crotons, hibiscus, codiaeum, and various ferns fills the pathway garden. A large terra-cotta jar holds water and lotus plants. Seating areas in garden rooms are arranged to make the most of the view. The terraced rice paddies, developed over hundreds of years of cultivation and water management, climb up the opposite hill like giant green steps.

15

WHITE/JAKOBS GARDEN

LONG ISLAND, NEW YORK

The David White and Robert Jakobs house is open to cross-breezes and views into the surrounding garden. Green swaths of lawn terminate in tall beech hedges. On either side, deep beds have lateral paths lined with mounds of boxwood. Beds are planted with tall stands of *Cimicifuga simplex* and *Macleaya cordata*, which seem to hang freely in the air. Below them tiger lilies, lysimachia, acanthus, dill, roses, phlox, and iris grow close together. On the front of the wood-shingled house, a heavy trellis supports climbing roses. House and garden seem to be all one, whether from within or without.

16

THE JOHN WHITWORTH GARDEN

MILLBROOK, NEW YORK

John Whitworth has views across the undulating hills of Dutchess County, which he has framed on either side with a collection of evergreen shrubs and trees. A mixture of thujas, arborvitae, and false cypresses is used to produce gradations of greens that are dramatic throughout the year. There are other rooms to the garden, with a hillside garden and Japanese-style plantings.

17

THE JOHN WHITWORTH GARDEN

A beautiful half-circle border opposite an entrance to the house is dug into a hillside with a dry-stone retaining wall behind it. A color-filled garden with wooden fencing is placed to benefit from the evergreen backdrop. The colors are hot from poppies, barberries and smoke trees, honeysuckle, marigolds, cannas, plume poppies, and hollyhocks. The garden as a whole is put together so that its various elements borrow from each other as well as from the surrounding landscape.

18

THE JOHN WHITWORTH GARDEN

MILLBROOK, NEW YORK

A detail of one of the yellow thujas shows the wonderful gradations of color there can be in a well-planted evergreen garden. Thujas are ideal for the bones of a garden, especially for creating rooms and sculpting shapes. Unfortunately, they are attractive food for deer in severe winters and will be eaten up to as high as a deer can reach, ruining the shape. Keeping deer out of a garden is essential, because once they have discovered a food source, they will keep returning to it.

19

A WILDFLOWER GARDEN

SOUTHAMPTON, NEW YORK

The flat, rich loam of Long Island is noted for its potato fields and, more recently, a burst of new houses and gardens. In the mid-1980s, a four-acre site with high privet hedges, whose previous use had been as a motorbike trail, was turned into a wildflower garden. Bruce Kelly and Galen Williams were commissioned, and garden rooms with connecting corridors were created by constant mowing. Garden furniture may complete a room, or simple statuary can add a formal element. The advantage of these loose rooms is that different ones can be utilized with moveable furniture and minimum effort.

20

A WILDFLOWER GARDEN

SOUTHAMPTON, NEW YORK

Wild and naturalized flowers include California and Shirley poppies, bachelor's buttons, black-eyed Susans, Queen Anne's lace, columbines, wild bleeding hearts, goldenrod, fleabane, asters, and many varieties of grasses. The wildflowers have their own blooming times and areas of interest, which change depending on what species is in predominance at different times.

A WILDFLOWER GARDEN

A more permanent gazebo for protection from the strong sun is surrounded by a sea of cleomes. A simple wooden fence delineating the more formal part of the garden closer to the house is planted with *Artemisia* 'Silver Queen,' whose color is a good bridge to the wildflower area. Wildflower gardens are deceptively difficult to grow, but offer an ever-changing combination of blooms for a whole season.

BUNNY WILLIAMS GARDEN

CONNECTICUT

Interior designer and garden writer Bunny Williams has creatively arranged her garden into several separate and distinct areas around her white wooden house. It does not take long to realize, when entering her driveway, that this is a serious garden, as green boxwood spheres lead your eye off to the front of the house. Morning light breaks through the mist, highlighting a cedar tree and the cobwebs on the boxwood balls.

23

BUNNY WILLIAMS GARDEN

CONNECTICUT

A central stairway graced with white hydrangeas leads to a sunken garden with a rectangular pool. On both sides there are deep and tall perennial borders. Moss-covered stone benches flank the pool, and on an axis to the stairs a wooden trellised opening in the hedge reveals a large terra-cotta jar. The garden works well when seen from inside the house, with strong lateral lines grounding it.

24

BUNNY WILLIAMS GARDEN

CONNECTICUT

On the opposite side of the house lies an intricately planted herb and vegetable garden facing a formal conservatory. A marble table in the conservatory looks out over the vegetable garden and can be decorated with an extensive collection of different potted auriculas. The interconnection of the garden and the conservatory has been well designed, down to the color of the paint trim on the large windows.

BUNNY WILLIAMS GARDEN
CONNECTICUT

The herbs and vegetables are arranged for companion planting in beds with dark-fired clay edgings and brick pathways. A rustic pergola runs down one side and supports various climbing vines. A stairway with stone slabs intergrown with santolina and accented with terra-cotta pots of helichrysum leads toward the greenhouse and cutting garden. Everywhere one turns there is detail, thought out and applied for color and form. It is a serious garden with a lighthearted feeling.

26

WING HAVEN

CHARLOTTE, NORTH CAROLINA

Wing Haven was the garden of Elizabeth and Edwin Clarkson and many of their feathered friends. The Clarksons would eat lunch together in the garden, the table impeccably dressed with a white cloth, and all around them birds would gather, flying up to take food directly out of their palms. Mrs. Clarkson had a clam-shaped silver pouch for carrying bird delights as she walked through the garden, which was started in 1927 with cuttings from Texas when Mrs. Clarkson came to the house as a new bride. It grew in bits and pieces as different plots of land were acquired, multiple rooms developed with strong, long axial paths crisscrossing this way and that. Box hedges skirt the paths, some of brick with grass in the center, some just grass. Camellia, mahonia, nandina, mock orange, and white Japanese quince were planted in the beds between the paths. Over wooden arches and in the trees, climbing roses, clematis, honeysuckle, trumpet vine, and *Elaeagnus pungens* give the garden a soft, enveloping style. Little nooks contain statues of saints, plaques of favorite verse, some ten birdbaths and pools. Benches everywhere look down the vistas. The garden is now owned by the Wing Haven Foundation.

27

PETER WOOSTER GARDEN

CONNECTICUT

The Peter Wooster garden sits on the edge of a soft valley that is kept as a meadow of grasses and wildflowers bordered with woodland. The garden is enclosed by a wooden trellis fence with two gates opposite each other on a central grass axis. When you enter the garden, you are enfolded by a botanical waterfall. Wooster is a master plantsman and noted for his color combinations. The garden has a cross-axis design with the central feature an octagonal wooden turret held high on a chestnut post.

28

PETER WOOSTER GARDEN
CONNECTICUT

There are several 360-degree beds jammed with plants that often grow eight feet tall. The color combinations work between neighboring plants and also between facing beds. The paths are closely cut grass, so the eye is captivated by plants that are so well tended they almost sing aloud. The fencing doubles as support for climbing roses, clematis, honeysuckle, and trumpet vine, *Campsis radicans.* \

PETER WOOSTER GARDEN

There are small features like a birdbath, a sundial, a central seating area, an obelisk, and antique benches, but what the garden is really about is plant happenings. There are special moments that plantsmen look forward to with expectation, as when *Rheum palmatum* 'Bowles Crimson' pushes up through a bed of ferns finally to flower, or when *Buddleia alternifolia* 'Argentea' is mixed with alliums and cotinus. Combinations like that do not mean much to most of us, but for the enthusiast these moments are eagerly awaited each year.

30

THE ABBIE ZABAR GARDEN

NEW YORK CITY

Manhattan rooftops are not known for natural beauty or easy growing conditions, but the views can be spectacular. Central Park is the backdrop for Abbie Zabar's topiary herb garden. Zabar is an artist, designer, and garden writer, and has written about her potted herbs and rooftop garden, revealing her intimate connection to them. The idea is simple but the execution exacting—a small topiary garden of mostly evergreens stays in place throughout the year. To make it even more functional, most of the topiaries are culinary herbs—including pine needle rosemary, sweet myrtle, bay, and lavender—all planted in terra-cotta pots and carefully pruned into spheres. As a backdrop, a yew hedge is flanked by junipers pruned into spiral forms. Within the apartment, arrangements of more topiaried herbs are placed in visual harmony with the outside garden. The idea is unique for a rooftop garden; its power comes from Zabar's design sense and her intense observation of every aspect, internal and external.

31

A ZELUN GARDEN

WOLONG, CHENGDU PROVINCE, CHINA

This Chinese vegetable garden contains the staple fare of cabbages and onions. Next to the door there is a single potted geranium, and a few flowers grace the bottom of the garden. Plants are held for drying on a shelf under the eaves and on the roof. Backpack baskets stand ready by the door.

INDEX

DIRECTORY OF PUBLIC GARDENS

ABKHAZI GARDEN
1964 Fairfield Road
Victoria, BC, V8S 1H4
Canada
(250) 598-8096

AGECROFT HALL
4305 Sulgrave Road
Richmond, Virginia 23221
(804) 353-4241
www.agecrofthall.com

BILTMORE ESTATE
1 Approach Road
Asheville, NC 28803
(800) 624-1575
www.Biltmore.com

CHICAGO BOTANIC GARDEN
1000 Lake Cook Road
Glencoe, IL 60022
(847) 835-5440
www.chicagobotanic.org

THE CLOISTERS
Fort Tryon Park
New York, NY 10040
(212) 923-3700

DUMBARTON OAKS
1703 32nd Street, NW
Washington, D.C. 20007
(202) 339-6401
www.doaks.org

THE ELMS
Newport Mansions
367 Bellevue Avenue
Newport, RI 02840
(401) 847-1000
www.newportmansions.org

EXBURY GARDENS
The Estate Office
Exbury, Southampton
Hampshire SO45 1AZ, UK
023 8089 9422
www.exbury.co.uk

**THE FELLS AT THE JOHN HAY
NATIONAL WILDLIFE REFUGE**
Route 103A
Newbury, New Hampshire 03255
(603) 763-4789
www.thefells.org

FILOLI CENTER
86 Cañada Road
Woodside, California 94062
(650) 364-8300
www.filoli.org

HATFIELD HOUSE
Hertfordshire
AL9 5NQ, UK
44 (0) 1707 287010
www.hatfield-house.co.uk

HERONSWOOD NURSERY
7530 NE 288th Street
Kingston, WA 98346
(360) 297-4172
www.heronswood.com

HIDCOTE GARDEN
Hidcote Bartrim,
nr Chipping Campden, England
GL55 6LR, NB
0044 (0) 1386 438333

**THE JOHN P. HUMES JAPANESE
STROLL GARDEN**
347 Oyster Bay Road
Millneck, NY 11560
(516) 676-4486

**THE HUNTINGTON LIBRARY,
ART COLLECTIONS,
AND BOTANICAL GARDENS**
1151 Oxford Road
San Marino, CA 91108
(626) 405-2100
www.huntington.org

INNISFREE GARDENS
Tyrrel Road
Millbrook, New York 12545
(845) 677-5286
www.innisfreegarden.com

**KYKUIT ESTATE,
THE ROCKEFELLER ESTATE**
Pocantico Hills
Tarrytown, New York 10591
(914) 631-9491
www.hudsonvalley.org

**LA PURISIMA MISSION
STATE HISTORIC PARK**
2295 Purisima Road
Lompoc, CA   93436
(805) 733-3713
www.lapurisimamission.org

LINCOLN MEMORIAL GARDEN
2301 East Lake Shore Drive
Springfield, IL 62707
(217) 529-1111
www.lmgnc.com

LOTUSLAND
695 Ashley Road
Santa Barbara, CA 93108
(805) 969-3767
www.lotusland.org

LYNDHURST
635 South Broadway
Tarrytown, NY 10591
(914) 631-4481
www.Lyndhurst.org

**MAGNOLIA PLANTATION
AND ITS GARDENS**
3550 Ashley River Road
Charleston, SC 29414
(843) 571.1266
www.magnoliaplantation.com

MIDDLETON PLACE
4300 Ashley River Road
Charleston, SC 29414
(800) 782-3608
www.middletonplace.org

MONTGOMERY PLACE
River Road
Annandale-on-Hudson, NY
(845) 758-5461
www.hudsonvalley.org

MONTICELLO
931 Thomas Jefferson Parkway
Charlottesville, VA 22902

MOTTISFONT ABBEY GARDEN
nr Romsey,
SO51 0LP, UK
0044(0)1794 341220 (Infoline)

MOUNT STEWART
Portaferry Road,
Newtownards,
BT22 2AD, N. Ireland
0044 (0) 28 4278 8387

NAUMKEAG
Prospect Hill Road
Stockbridge, MA
(413) 298.3239

THE NEW YORK BOTANIC GARDEN
Bronx River Parkway
at Fordham Road
Bronx, NY 10458
(718) 817-8700
www.nybg.org

**NÔTRE DAME ABBEY
LE BEC HELLOUIN**
27800 Le Bec-Hellouin, France
02 32 43 72 60
www.abbayedubec.com

OLD WESTBURY
71 Old Westbury Road
Old Westbury, NY 11568
(516) 333-0048
www.oldwestburygardens.org

PLIMOTH PLANTATION
137 Warren Avenue
Plymouth, MA 02360
(508) 746-1622
www.plimoth.org

**THE JOHN AND MABLE RINGLING
MUSEUM OF ART**
5401 Bay Shore Road
Sarasota, Florida 34243
(941) 359-5700
www.ringling.org

**ROSEDOWN PLANTATION
STATE HISTORIC SITE**
12501 Louisiana Highway 10
St. Francisville, LA 70775
(225) 635-3332 or 1-888-376-
1867

**ROUSHAM PARK
HOUSE AND GARDEN**
Steeple Aston
Bicester
Oxfordshire
OX25 4QX, UK
+44 (0)1869 347 110

SANTA BARBARA BOTANIC GARDEN
1212 Mission Canyon Road
Santa Barbara, CA 93105
(805) 682-4726
www.santabarbarabotanicgarden.org

STATEN ISLAND BOTANIC GARDEN
1000 Richmond Terrace
Staten Island, NY 10301
www.sibg.org
(718) 273-8200

ST. MARY AT LAMBETH
Lambeth Palace Road
London SE1 7LB, England
020 7401 8865
www.museumgardenhistory.org

STONECROP GARDENS
81 Stonecrop Lane
Cold Spring, NY 10516
845-265-2000
www.stonecrop.org

STOURHEAD
Stourhead Estate Office,
Stourton,
Warminster,
BA12 6QD, UK
0044 (0) 1747 841152

TINTINHULL
Farm Street,
Tintinhull,
Yeovil,
BA22 9PZ, UK
0044 (0) 1935 822545

UPTON HOUSE AND GARDEN
nr Banbury,
OX15 6HT, UK
0044(0)1295 670266

VANDERBILT MANSION
4097 Albany Post Road
Hyde Park, NY 12538
845 229-9115
www.nps.gov

VIZCAYA MUSEUM AND GARDENS
3251 South Miami Avenue
Miami, Florida 33129
(305) 250.9133
www.vizcayamuseum.org

WAVE HILL
675 West 252 Street
Bronx, NY 10471
(718) 549-3200
www.wavehill.org

WESTERN HILLS NURSERY
16250 Coleman Valley Road
Occidental, CA 95465-9229
(707) 874-37371

**WINGHAVEN GARDENS AND BIRD
SANCTUARY**
248 Ridgewood Avenue
Charlotte, North Carolina 28209
(704) 331-0664
www.winghavengardens.com

ACKNOWLEDGMENTS

I thank God for the opportunity to create this book.

Countless thanks to my gorgeous wife, Christine Simoneau Hales, who encouraged, supported, and worked many hours herself on this project.

Many thanks to the editorial direction of Margaret L. Kaplan, the writing and gardening knowledge of Denise Otis, the arduous work of Jon Cipriaso and Audrey Wyman.

Sincere thanks to all the garden owners who allowed me to photograph their gardens over the years, especially those included in this book.

A special thanks to Frank Cabot for his preface and his contributions to the gardening world.

FRONT COVER, FRONTISPIECE, PAGE 6
The Alhambra and Generalife Gardens, Granada, Spain

BACK COVER
Huntington Botanical Gardens, San Marino, California

PAGE 5: Stonecrop Gardens, Cold Spring, New York
PAGE 7: Hidcote Manor Garden, Gloucestershire, England

Photographs © Mick Hales

Editor: Margaret L. Kaplan
Editorial Assistant: Jon Cipriaso
Consulting Editor: Denise Otis
Designer: Eric Baker Design Associates, Eric Janssen Strohl
Production Manager: Maria Pia Gramaglia

Library of Congress Cataloging-in-Publication Data

Hales, Michael.
   Gardens around the world : 365 days / by Mick Hales.
      p. cm.
Includes bibliographical references and index.
   ISBN 0-8109-4980-6 (hardcover)
   1. Gardens. I. Title.

SB451.H36 2004
712—dc22

                                    2003024832

Copyright © Mick Hales

Printed and bound in China

10 9 8 7 6 5 4 3 2

Harry N. Abrams, Inc.
100 Fifth Avenue
New York, N.Y. 10011
www.abramsbooks.com

Abrams is a subsidiary of

LA MARTINIÈRE
GROUPE